I0644668

Virtual Reality Therapy in the Metaverse

Virtual Reality Therapy in the Metaverse provides mental health practitioners with a comprehensive, evidence-based guide to integrating virtual reality (VR) into psychotherapeutic practice. From preparing patients and obtaining informed consent to selecting hardware and designing virtual exposure environments, this book translates a growing body of research into practical clinical guidance.

The book equips clinicians with the knowledge needed to navigate every stage of VR integration. It begins with the preparatory steps – building the therapeutic alliance, obtaining informed consent and identifying appropriate patients – before examining the ethical, logistical and technological considerations involved in delivering VR-based interventions. Detailed chapters apply VR to the three pillars of cognitive behavioural therapy: exposure-based desensitisation, cognitive restructuring and skills training. Case examples show how virtual environments can be individually tailored to treat conditions ranging from contamination OCD to treatment-resistant auditory hallucinations. The final section looks ahead, reviewing hardware and software advances and presenting a four-phase roadmap from augmented reality to psychotherapy in a fully realised metaverse.

Virtual Reality Therapy in the Metaverse is intended for practising psychotherapists, psychiatrists, psychologists, counsellors and trainees, as well as researchers and technology developers working at the intersection of mental health and immersive technology.

Bruce Bassi, M.S., M.D., is board-certified in psychiatry and addiction psychiatry. He earned his M.S. in biomedical engineering from Columbia University and his M.D. from the University of Michigan. He is the founder of TelepsychHealth, a multi-state telehealth psychiatry practice, and the founder/CEO of My Medical Records Inc., a healthcare AI company designed for patients, providers and organisations.

The Metaverse

The Metaverse: A Critical Introduction
David Burden and Maggi Savin-Baden

The Metaverse for Learning and Education
Maggi Savin-Baden and David Burden

The Military Metaverse
Andy Fawkes and David Burden

Cities in the Metaverse: Spatial Computing, Digital Twins, Avatars, Economics and Digital Habitation on the New Frontier
Andrew Hudson-Smith, Duncan Wilson and Valerio Signorelli

Virtual Reality Therapy in the Metaverse: A Clinician's Guide to Getting Started with Virtual Reality-Based Psychotherapy
Bruce Bassi

For more information about this series please visit: www.routledge.com/The-Metaverse/book-series/

Virtual Reality Therapy in the Metaverse

A Clinician's Guide to Getting Started with Virtual Reality-Based Psychotherapy

Bruce Bassi

CRC Press
Taylor & Francis Group
Boca Raton London New York

CRC Press is an imprint of the
Taylor & Francis Group, an **informa** business
A CHAPMAN & HALL BOOK

Designed cover image: Shutterstock

First edition published 2027
by CRC Press
2385 NW Executive Center Drive, Suite 320, Boca Raton FL 33431

and by CRC Press
4 Park Square, Milton Park, Abingdon, Oxon, OX14 4RN

CRC Press is an imprint of Taylor & Francis Group, LLC

ISBN: 978-1-032-55936-0 (hbk)
ISBN: 978-1-032-55935-3 (pbk)
ISBN: 978-1-003-43297-5 (ebk)

DOI: 10.1201/b23370

Typeset in Palatino
by Newgen Publishing UK

To my kids, Theo and Noah, and their boundless interest in technology,

just like their father.

Contents

Preface ix
Acknowledgements xi
List of Figures and Tables xiii
Introduction xv

Part 1 Principles of the Metaverse Applied to Psychotherapy

1 Preparation 3

2 Service Delivery 16

3 Ethical Considerations 25

4 Metaverse Elements 31

5 Physical Components 36

6 Virtual Environments 44

Part 2 Applied Models for VR Psychotherapy

7 Cue/Sensory Desensitisation 53

8 Cognitive Training 74

9 Skills Training 95

Part 3 Future Directions of Psychotherapy in the Metaverse

10 Hardware Improvements 111

11 Software Improvements 119

12 Roadmap for Clinical Practice 124

References 133

Index 149

Preface

I was fortunate to practise medicine in the years before telehealth became commonplace. Back then, many people, including my colleagues, viewed it with suspicion: it felt odd, impersonal, even "less than" an in-office visit. The data told a different story. Telehealth was already proving just as effective for psychiatric care, but it took a global pandemic for the field to finally embrace it. Once the public began using it, the conversation changed. Scepticism gave way to familiarity, and what once seemed strange quickly became standard care.

Virtual reality (VR) therapy stands today exactly where telehealth stood in 2019.

I don't believe another worldwide crisis will force its adoption. This time, the surge will have to come from us: clinicians willing to try it, adapt it and talk about it openly.

Right now, VR therapy faces an uphill battle. Beyond the usual misconceptions and unfamiliarity, most clinicians were never trained to use it. We're taught to master the basics first, and VR is presented as an afterthought, a "nice-to-have" tool to try only after everything else has failed. It is rarely discussed as a first-line intervention. The reasons are practical and familiar: the initial cost of hardware, lack of standardised training programmes, uncertain insurance reimbursement and the lingering perception that it is somehow gimmicky or experimental.

Again, the data tell a compellingly different story. Multiple meta-analyses show that VR exposure therapy produces large effect sizes for specific phobias, often equal to or greater than traditional *in vivo* exposure. Strong evidence also supports its use in PTSD, social anxiety disorder and panic disorder. Patients habituate faster, dropout rates are lower and many describe the experience as more tolerable than imagined.

Given this mismatch between evidence and everyday practice, one has to ask: why isn't VR therapy used more widely? The answer, as we saw with telehealth, is less about the technology itself and more about societal acceptance, familiarity and professional comfort.

It's fascinating how much our collective willingness to try something new shapes its destiny. Like a mattress, VR has a "you have to try it first" problem. Once therapists and patients actually put on the headset, the usual reaction is the same: "Why isn't everyone doing this?"

The good news is that the technology itself has crossed a tipping point. Visual fidelity has increased substantially, and the integration of highly intelligent AI has removed the last major limitations. Instead of being confined to a small library of generic environments, generative AI can now create or modify scenes on the fly based on a patient's exact description: an idiosyncratic trauma memory, a specific social scenario, even a childhood fear that defies standard templates. Real-time AI can monitor physiological signals and adapt the intensity of the experience with greater precision and less latency than any human therapist could manage manually. Between sessions, AI coaching can reinforce lessons, track progress and deliver concise reports to the clinician. An AI co-pilot could eventually support human therapists in the room, offering real-time suggestions and decision support based on data.

This book exists to show that the barriers to entry into the world of VR therapy are far lower than most clinicians believe. As Chapter 5 describes, a stand-alone VR headset capable of immersive therapy now costs under $500, and Chapter 12 outlines how clinicians can take their first step into extended reality using nothing more than a smartphone-based augmented reality application. Much like telehealth before COVID, the tools are now accessible to the average therapist.

The book is organised around core principles of cognitive behavioural therapy that apply across diagnoses, so clinicians trained in evidence-based practice already possess the clinical foundation they need. Part 1 lays the groundwork: how to prepare patients, obtain informed consent, navigate the ethical landscape and select hardware and software suited to your practice. Part 2 is the clinical heart of the book, structured around the three pillars of cognitive behavioural therapy: cue and sensory desensitisation (Chapter 7), cognitive training (Chapter 8) and skills training (Chapter 9). I chose this structure deliberately. Rather than organising by diagnosis, which would force readers to hunt for relevant techniques across scattered chapters, organising by therapeutic mechanism means that a clinician trained in CBT already has the conceptual scaffolding to apply VR across anxiety disorders, PTSD, OCD, substance use disorders, eating disorders, psychotic disorders, depression and autism spectrum disorders. Part 3 looks ahead, examining the hardware and software innovations on the horizon and offering a phased roadmap for integrating extended reality into your practice, wherever you are starting from.

My hope is that this book helps move VR therapy from the margins to the mainstream, where the evidence already says it belongs. And if you're reading this and feeling sceptical about new technology, you are precisely the person we need to be more involved. History shows that the most thoughtful ethical frameworks come from those willing to engage with the change rather than dismiss it. The telephone was once called "the instrument of the devil" for supposedly destroying face-to-face conversation and threatening privacy. We have heard these concerns before. Let's shape this technology wisely, together.

Acknowledgements

I would like to thank Maggi Savin-Baden for giving me the opportunity to write this book, as well as David Burden for his assistance in editing. I would also like to thank the several clinicians who helped me understand how they use VR in practice, as well as their recommendations for best practices: Dr. Kim Bullock, Myron Dianiska, LPC, Dr. Paul Greenfield, Dr. Howard Gurr, Dr. Elizabeth McMahon and Tiffany Song, LCSW.

Figures and Tables

Figures

2.1 Adoption readiness model: From telehealth to VR to metaverse 18
4.1 How metaverse elements interact to influence therapeutic outcomes 32
7.1 The anxiety-avoidance cycle perpetuates anxiety 54
7.2 CBT thinking error cycle demonstrating how distorted thoughts, negative emotions and misinterpreted physical symptoms perpetuate maladaptive behaviours 55
9.1 Behavioural activation worksheet demonstrates the impact of behavioural activation on mood and sense of achievement 107
11.1 Biofeedback-driven dynamic environment loop 122

Tables

1.1 Psychotherapy concepts, descriptions and potential VR applications 8
1.2 Clinical checklist – VR indications and contraindications 14
2.1 Barriers and solutions – Telehealth vs. VR psychotherapy 23
3.1 Ethical considerations framework for VR psychotherapy 26
5.1 Descriptions, applications and examples of VR, AR and MR 37
5.2 VR platforms summarising special features and prices 39
5.3 Summary of device, type of data collected, sensor type and information provided 41
6.1 VE type, description, advantages and disadvantages 48
7.1 Summary of Part 2 content 52
7.2 Summary of diagnostic category, fear and exposure concepts 59
7.3 Summary of VR exposure therapy evidence by disorder 72
8.1 Example CBT thought record used in cognitive restructuring: identifying negative automatic thoughts, generating alternative thoughts and re-rating mood 75
10.1 Summary of tracking type with description, advantages and disadvantages 114
12.1 Roadmap summary: Phases, technologies, clinical applications and prerequisites 125

Introduction

What is the metaverse? The term is often used without any context, so accurately defining it can be a challenge. Imagine trying to describe the internet, with all its current functionality, to someone in the 1970s when the idea of the internet existed, but it had not yet been fully realised. Trying to define the metaverse while it is still being developed is similarly difficult.

The term "metaverse" was first found in Neal Stephenson's 1992 science fiction novel *Snow Crash*. The word is formed by combining the Greek word "meta," which means transcendence or transformation, with "universe," to reflect the world of human experience. For this book, the metaverse refers to the vast virtual environment that exists alongside the physical world and within which people interact through digital avatars (Lee, 2023).

Virtual reality (VR) is an integral part of the metaverse as it enables users to interact with one another and with elements present in the virtual environment. The purpose of this book is to consider how the metaverse can impact psychotherapy, with a specific focus on VR-based interventions. In addition to introducing readers to VR, augmented and mixed reality and the metaverse, this book will focus on how these technologies can impact psychotherapy.

The first part of this book describes these technologies and how they can be applied to psychotherapy in general. Part 1 explores how extended reality technologies can impact the psychotherapeutic process and provides guidance for mental health practitioners looking to incorporate this technology, including ethical considerations. Part 1 concludes with a discussion of the physical components of VR, virtual environments and how to compare VR platforms for psychotherapy.

The second part of this book focuses on how VR can be applied to psychotherapy for specific mental health conditions. This part is divided into three chapters that apply VR to three components of cognitive behavioural therapy (CBT): cue/sensory desensitisation via exposure therapy, cognitive training and skills training. Research investigating the efficacy of VR-based interventions for anxiety disorders, obsessive compulsive disorder (OCD), post-traumatic stress disorder (PTSD), substance use disorders, depression, autism spectrum disorders, psychotic disorders and eating disorders is presented. In addition, case examples highlight how VR can be applied to specific patients.

In the third part of this book, the future of psychotherapy in the metaverse is examined, including a description of the hardware and software improvements that would increase the utility of VR for psychotherapy. Finally, we give a roadmap of how extended reality technologies might be implemented into clinical practice and conclude with a speculation of what psychotherapy in the metaverse might eventually look like.

This book aims to equip psychotherapists with the knowledge and tools to navigate the evolving landscape of mental health care in the metaverse. By exploring the potential of VR and other extended reality technologies, I challenge readers to rethink traditional therapeutic approaches and embrace the possibilities of this new frontier. As the metaverse continues to develop, it is crucial for mental health professionals to remain informed and adaptable, ensuring they can provide effective and ethical care to clients in this virtual realm.

Part 1

Principles of the Metaverse Applied to Psychotherapy

Introduction

VR has tremendous potential to enhance psychotherapeutic interventions for a range of mental health conditions. VR allows patients to be immersed in highly realistic, multisensory environments tailored to their specific needs. Virtual environments provide patients with a safe space to confront their fears, challenge and replace maladaptive perceptions and beliefs and learn and practise new skills. The therapeutic possibilities of VR are nearly limitless; however, like any other intervention, clinicians must have a firm grasp on how to use this technology to best benefit their patients.

It is imperative to remember that VR is a tool to be used by experienced therapists within an established therapeutic relationship; it is not a replacement for therapists or the extensive training necessary for implementing effective treatment. Before integrating VR into clinical practice, it is essential that therapists have competence and experience with treating specific mental health concerns.

In the first half of Part 1, a framework for clinicians considering integrating VR into their clinical practice is presented. This part considers how VR can impact various aspects of therapy, including the therapeutic relationship, the efficacy of interventions and how clinicians can differentiate when and with which patients VR is likely to help. This section highlights the importance of honing clinical skills, developing a strong therapeutic relationship and

DOI: 10.1201/b23370-1

properly introducing VR-based interventions to patients, including obtaining informed consent. The integration of VR into clinical practice is compared to the shift to telehealth and remote psychotherapy. Furthermore, the ethical considerations of VR-based interventions are presented.

The second half of Part 1 focuses on VR technology. The physical components of VR are described, including currently available VR systems, VR accessories and biofeedback devices to enhance psychotherapeutic interventions. The differences between video-based and computer-generated virtual environments are discussed, and elements of the Metaverse (e.g., avatars, presence, immersion) that impact psychotherapy are presented. Part 1 concludes with a discussion of how to compare different VR systems and platforms to select the best fit for your clinical practice.

1

Preparation

Introduction

As with any psychotherapeutic intervention, considerable preparation is required before implementing VR into clinical practice. VR should only be implemented within an established therapeutic relationship, and many steps are involved before using the technology. Therapists must first feel comfortable with their non-VR-based clinical skills. They must have already built a strong therapeutic relationship within which they can raise the possibility of using VR-based interventions, educate the patient on how and why these interventions are recommended and explain how VR will be added to the therapy process. Therapists must also ensure that they have their patients' full informed consent. Additionally, the therapist must consider whether VR is indicated or contraindicated for specific patients.

Your Therapy Skills

Incorporating VR into therapy sessions can offer unique opportunities and benefits for your patients. It is important to remember, however, that therapists must hone their therapy skills before incorporating VR into their sessions, and there are several reasons for doing so. First, therapists must have a solid foundation in traditional therapy techniques and interventions before incorporating VR. The ability to manage potential risks in a VR environment is crucial, as a VR environment introduces new considerations and potential risks in therapy. By refining their therapy skills, therapists are better able to navigate technical challenges in real-time. Therapists must also assess and address their patients' needs and provide the appropriate support both in and out of a VR context.

DOI: 10.1201/b23370-2

Second, incorporating VR into therapeutic interventions is more than just using the technology itself. By honing your therapy skills, you can develop the clinical judgment needed to determine whether, when and how to incorporate VR into your sessions with a patient. Effective therapy involves tailoring the therapeutic interventions to meet the specific needs of each patient, and, thus, therapists must be prepared with a thorough understanding of their patients' responses and reactions to adapt VR interventions accordingly. Therapists must also understand how to integrate VR into their own personal therapeutic approach, ensuring that it aligns with their theoretical orientation. VR in therapy does not make you a better therapist; rather, it provides you with an additional tool to use with your patients. VR is not the treatment, but an adjunct to the treatment that can enhance the therapy.

Therapeutic Relationships

As previously mentioned, therapists should have a well-established rapport with their patients before incorporating VR interventions. As mental health symptoms can present differently in the metaverse, therapists should be prepared for various manifestations of symptoms. Mental health symptoms may present differently in VR therapy due to a variety of factors, such as the patient's comfort level with VR in general and his/her perceived anonymity in the metaverse. For example, a patient presenting with social anxiety who is comfortable in the metaverse may exhibit fewer or less severe symptoms in a VR environment. They may more easily maintain virtual conversations and be more open to exploring crowded virtual spaces. A patient presenting with social anxiety who is not comfortable in the metaverse may exhibit heightened symptoms of social anxiety in a virtual environment compared to a non-virtual environment. In this context, they might struggle to initiate or maintain virtual conversations, avoid overly crowded virtual spaces or exhibit avoidance in social interactions. It is also possible that they might experience virtual environments as more chaotic, threatening or overwhelming.

A patient's perceived anonymity and the presence of stigma during VR therapeutic interventions can greatly alter how their mental health symptoms present in the metaverse. Anonymity in the metaverse can influence a patient's open expression, disclosure of experiences and sense of safety. For example, the metaverse may create an environment where individuals feel more comfortable expressing their thoughts, feelings and experiences. A greater sense of anonymity may also encourage patients to disclose experiences that they may have otherwise been hesitant to share. They may be more willing to share sensitive information, promoting a deeper exploration and understanding of their mental health struggles.

The use of VR in therapeutic interventions may influence how patients perceive stigma in their own treatment. For example, the metaverse may provide a level of detachment from their physical appearance and real-world identity, providing them with a sense of reduced visibility. This sense of obscurity could reduce the potential for judgment, which may alleviate the feelings of stigma a patient seeking therapy for their mental health concerns might experience (Matsangidou et al., 2020). On the other hand, VR may lead patients to engage in digital self-preservation. In the metaverse, individuals can create their own avatars to represent themselves however they want in a virtual world. This creates room for concealing parts of themselves that they may be ashamed of or wish they could change. This can present as a hindrance to therapy as patients may not present as their true selves in a virtual environment.

Another option therapists may consider when incorporating VR into therapeutic interventions is co-therapy with another therapist. There are many benefits to choosing this route. Co-therapy can provide enhanced expertise, increased safety and allow for diverse yet complementary therapeutic styles and interventions. Co-therapists can bring diverse perspectives and insights to the therapeutic process, contributing to a more comprehensive understanding of a patient's needs and tailoring their therapy accordingly. This can be particularly useful in the metaverse, as different therapists can provide different areas of specialisation, therapeutic approaches and cultural perspectives. Having multiple therapists in the metaverse can also enhance the support and safety that is experienced by patients. For example, co-therapists can provide a greater sense of reassurance, stability and comfort for patients. Lastly, diverse yet complementary therapeutic styles and modalities can offer flexible therapy to meet individual patient needs and preferences, which can enhance the overall effectiveness and relevance of interventions.

Co-therapy may present some challenges as well. Co-therapists must ensure they have clear communication channels and provide seamless coordination during sessions. This may prove to be more difficult in the metaverse, as technical issues and virtual space management can arise. Additionally, co-therapists must establish clear roles, boundaries and mutual respect with one another before engaging in a VR co-therapeutic venture. The therapeutic alliance must be maintained, and it is crucial that patients feel comfortable with and equally supported by both therapists. Due to the potential benefits and limitations of co-therapy with another therapist, this practice should be carefully considered, and the decision should be made with the patient's best interests in mind.

The Therapeutic Alliance

The therapeutic relationship, or the alliance between the therapist and the patient, is a fundamental part of therapy. Nothing is more powerful than this relationship (Falkenström et al., 2013; Flückiger et al., 2018; Norcross, 2001; Weck et al., 2015). The therapeutic relationship is built upon trust, safety,

TABLE 1.1

Psychotherapy concepts, descriptions and potential VR applications

Concept	Description	VR Application
Exposure Therapy	Gradual exposure to situations, objects or memories that cause intense fear, anxiety or distress	VR creates realistic and safe environments to gradually confront and engage with fears in a controlled manner to promote habituation and new learning
Cognitive Behavioural Therapy (CBT)	Identify and modify unhelpful thoughts, beliefs and behaviours	VR enables interactive scenarios to challenge distorted thinking patterns and practise new, healthier coping strategies
Pain Management	Distraction techniques redirect attention away from pain sensations	VR blocks out the external world and immerses patients in calming and naturalistic environments to trigger endorphin release and analgesic effects
Social Skills Training	Learn and practise recognising and responding to social cues, improve social communication and emotion regulation in social settings	VR simulates social situations to allow patients to develop and practise social skills in a realistic and safe environment
Mindfulness	Focus attention on the present moment, increase non-judgmental thinking and acceptance, promote compassion and self-love	VR produces auditory and visual cues that promote focus and present moment awareness while blocking out the external world
Relaxation and Stress Reduction	Diaphragmatic breathing, progressive muscle relaxation and visualisation exercises promote relaxation and decrease stress	VR produces immersive and calming environments to block out the external world and enhance relaxation and stress reduction

VR technology creates a realistic and immersive environment for patients that can simulate various scenarios. These virtual environments are tailored to the patient's specific fear or phobia. For example, a patient with a fear of flying could experience a virtual airplane cabin with all the sights, sounds and turbulence simulations. This virtual environment can be controlled and manipulated by the therapist to allow for safe exposure to the feared stimuli and allow for a gradual increase in the level of exposure and difficulty over time. This allows patients to confront their fears in a supportive and encouraging environment, reducing the potential risk of overwhelming anxiety or trauma reactivation.

Cognitive-Behavioural Therapy

CBT is a common therapeutic technique that focuses on identifying and modifying unhelpful thoughts, beliefs and behaviours. The use of

VR in CBT can help by creating interactive scenarios that challenge a patient's distorted thinking patterns and facilitate the practice of new, healthier coping skills and behavioural changes. VR offers a dynamic and immersive platform in which a patient can learn, practise and apply CBT techniques.

For example, a patient with social anxiety may believe that they are always being judged negatively by others. This distorted perception can lead to avoidance behaviours, reinforcing their fears and limiting social interactions. Engaging in VR psychotherapy can create behavioural experiments in which they interact with other virtual avatars and challenge these negative beliefs.

Pain Management

VR can provide a distraction from pain and can produce an analgesic effect for individuals experiencing chronic pain or discomfort. Virtual environments can help patients redirect their attention away from pain sensations, thereby providing relief from chronic pain. Additionally, VR has been found to reduce the perception of pain intensity in patients, showing that VR can have an analgesic effect. The immersive and engaging nature scenes offered in VR can trigger the release of endorphins in the patient, creating a relaxation response and alleviating pain.

Social Skills Training

Social skills training via VR can provide a realistic social simulation that mimics real-life social situations that a patient may experience. These situations include, but are not limited to, job interviews, public speaking events or large social gatherings. Patients also have the opportunity to engage in and practise behaviour rehearsal and role-playing. VR can be used to enhance social skills training for patients with various mental health struggles, such as those on the autism spectrum or who suffer from social anxiety (Parsons and Mitchell, 2002). VR can simulate realistic social interactions and allow patients to practise recognising social cues, improve communication skills and work on emotional regulation in a controlled environment. VR offers patients a safe space for continued practice and feedback.

Mindfulness

VR can provide visual and auditory cues that promote relaxation, focus and present-moment awareness. This can enhance mindfulness and meditation practices for patients by enabling them to disconnect from the external world and immerse themselves in serene and tranquil virtual settings. Mindfulness practices in virtual environments allow patients to follow a virtual instructor who guides them through various techniques, including breath awareness, body scanning or loving-kindness meditation. VR has the potential to deepen the mindfulness experience and therefore provide greater effects for patients (Seabrook et al., 2020).

Relaxation and Stress Reduction

For relaxation and stress reduction, VR can be used to create immersive and calming environments. For example, VR environments can simulate peaceful landscapes or nature scenes, providing the patient with a visual and auditory approach to engaging in stress reduction techniques. A VR platform can also offer an interactive experience that guides individuals through deep breathing, progressive muscle relaxation and visualisations. Patients can choose from a variety of virtual environments, soundscapes and/or meditation styles based on their preferences and what works best for them. Utilising VR in relaxation and stress reduction techniques can be beneficial for managing stress, anxiety and promoting overall well-being in patients.

Obtaining Informed Consent

After discussing VR with their therapist, a patient may choose to incorporate it into their therapy sessions. Should this be the case, then appropriate consent must be obtained before moving forward. Informed consent includes a thorough discussion of potential side effects and risks associated with VR. The potential side effects include, but are not limited to:

- motion sickness and discomfort
- eye strain or visual discomfort
- VR dependence
- post-VR disorientation
- privacy concerns

Motion Sickness and Discomfort

Some individuals may experience motion sickness, dizziness or discomfort when using VR technology. The intensity of these symptoms can greatly vary depending on the individual and can also vary from use to use. The quality of the VR technology and the content being observed can also contribute to sickness, dizziness and/or discomfort.

Eye Strain and Visual Discomfort

Prolonged use of VR headsets may cause the patient to experience eye strain, fatigue or temporary visual disturbances. These effects may be caused by the close proximity of the VR headset to the eyes and the constant adjustment of focus between near and far objects.

VR Dependence

Excessive use of VR technology can pose a risk of creating dependence on virtual experiences. If an individual begins to prefer virtual experiences over real-world experiences, they may choose to interact with others solely in a virtual environment, creating a dependency. Additionally, excessive use of VR may lead to reduced social interactions and create isolation from real-world relationships. This can hinder social skills development.

Post-VR Disorientation

Some individuals may experience a temporary disorientation or confusion after a VR session as they readjust to their physical environment. This is known as the "post-VR effect" or "VR hangover." This phenomenon can lead to feelings of detachment, altered perceptions of space or a brief delay when readapting to the real world.

Privacy Concerns

The collection and storage of user data often raise privacy and security concerns. Therapists and patients should be mindful of what permissions they are granting and ensure they are using trusted platforms that prioritise data protection. Privacy concerns will be addressed in more detail in the section covering ethical considerations.

VR Homework

Using VR to practise therapeutic skills outside of a therapy setting can be a controversial topic. For instance, VR homework can be a valuable tool to enhance therapy outcomes by providing the opportunity to reinforce and practise skills learned in therapy. VR homework can also be beneficial to patients as it increases the generalisability of skills learned in a therapy setting to real-world contexts. For example, it can allow patients to work on VR settings in a different context, such as without the therapist present. This increases the likelihood of sustained improvement and positive outcomes. Furthermore, VR homework can provide valuable insight into a patient's progress. For example, therapists can collect objective measurements, such as physiological responses, to assess progress and adjust treatment plans accordingly.

VR homework has potential challenges or limitations as well. VR homework may create an adverse reaction, exacerbation of symptoms or cause extreme distress in patients. Therapists should therefore evaluate the patient's clinical progress, symptom stability and demonstrated mastery of relevant coping skills in session before assigning VR homework independently. If issues arise, the patient will not be in a setting in which they can receive immediate therapeutic support. Another potential limitation is engagement in VR homework. Some patients may have personal preferences or comfort levels that influence their willingness to engage in VR homework. Therapists should consider individual preferences and readiness when assigning VR homework and be prepared to provide alternative options if necessary.

When assigning VR homework, therapists should provide clear instructions, guidelines and support for patients. Regular check-ins, debriefing sessions and/or progress reviews can help patients process their experiences and receive further guidance from their therapist. Therapists should have a plan in place if their patient experiences extreme distress from their VR homework and the patient should be aware of and agree to this plan. Therapists must ensure that the VR homework assignments are appropriate, safe and aligned with the patient's treatment goals.

Indications

Incorporating VR in a therapeutic setting can be useful for a variety of mental health concerns (Table 1.2). Research has shown that VR-based interventions have been effective in the treatment of anxiety disorders, PTSD, pain management, phobia and fear-related disorders, obsessive-compulsive disorder (OCD), autism spectrum disorder (ASD), eating disorders, substance use disorders, depression and mood disorders, psychotic disorders and body image and self-esteem issues (Difede et al., 2007; Ferrer-Garcia et al., 2017; Freeman et al., 2016; Krijn et al., 2004; Laforest et al., 2016; Parsons and Mitchell, 2002; Pourmand, 2018; Taubin et al., 2022; Weschler et al., 2019).

VR allows patients to gradually confront and manage their fears in a safe and controlled setting that allows the patient to focus on cue or sensory desensitisation. For patients with anxiety disorders or PTSD, VR has been utilised in treatment with patients to facilitate exposure therapy. VR therapy is useful in treating phobias and fear-related disorders by creating virtual environments that replicate phobic stimuli. As such, therapists can gradually expose their patients to feared objects, leading to desensitisation and reduced anxiety response.

VR is suitable for therapeutic approaches involving cognitive training, such as for pain management. VR therapeutic interventions can facilitate relaxation responses in patients experiencing chronic pain. Moreover, a virtual environment can be designed in a therapeutic setting to address and combat feelings of body dissatisfaction, body dysmorphia and/or negative self-perceptions. Patients can practise activities that increase self-acceptance and positive self-talk in a VR setting.

VR works well for disorders requiring focus on skills development and retraining. For patients with ASD, VR can be used as a tool to practise social skills training by simulating social situations and allowing patients to practise their abilities. In the treatment of eating disorders, VR in a therapeutic setting can be used to simulate scenarios that involve meals or challenging eating situations so that patients may practise utilising coping strategies or challenging distorted thoughts in these scenarios. In patients suffering from substance use disorders, a virtual environment can recreate situations that can trigger cravings and allow patients to practise coping skills and refusal strategies.

VR in a therapeutic setting for depression and mood disorders can offer positive, virtual experiences promoting relaxation and positive thinking. VR can deliver immersive environments for mindfulness and CBT, allowing patients to confront and manage negative emotions in a controlled and safe space. This can be used to enhance mood, increase motivation and provide a sense of accomplishment in patients.

In general, individual preferences and circumstances may predict the likelihood of participation in VR therapy. Individuals who are more tech savvy, already familiar with VR or more open to technology are more likely to be interested in incorporating VR into their therapy sessions. Patients who are open to innovative approaches to therapy are more likely to engage in VR in their treatment. Lastly, patients who are in a clinical setting or have the personal means for VR equipment and associated costs have a greater likelihood of participating in VR therapy.

Contraindications

While research has shown many benefits of incorporating VR in a therapeutic setting, there are contraindications that should also be considered. It is possible that a VR setting can cause severe motion sickness or simulator sickness. Some patients may experience significant levels of discomfort, dizziness, nausea or motion sickness when using this technology, and this may inadvertently worsen symptoms. Additionally, patients experiencing a headache may find a short-term worsening of symptoms. For patients who have epilepsy or are at an increased risk of seizures, a virtual environment could potentially be harmful. VR environments that involve intense visual or auditory stimuli, rapid movements or flashing lights have the possibility of triggering seizures in individuals who have a history of seizures or epilepsy. Careful consideration and precautions should be taken if a VR therapeutic intervention is being considered for these patients.

Patients with sensory sensitivities or disorders may be particularly sensitive to visual and/or auditory stimuli. As such, a VR environment may overload their sensory system and cause significant distress. For instance, a patient with a low-grade vestibular dysfunction could feel disequilibrium or have an adverse reaction to the physiological reaction simulated in VR therapy. Careful assessment should be carried out before utilising VR in therapy with patients with sensory sensitivities.

VR therapy may not be a suitable first-choice modality for acutely unstable psychiatric conditions, such as new onset psychosis, mania, suicidal ideation or PTSD symptoms. Therapists should consider stabilising the acute phase of illness and developing patient insight into the condition before incorporating VR. Immersive VR environments can be intense and may exacerbate symptoms or cause distress or dissociation. Furthermore, if a patient suffering from PTSD has a history of adverse reactions to trauma reminders, careful consideration should be made before using VR technology in therapy.

TABLE 1.2

Clinical checklist – VR indications and contraindications

Category	Indications (Consider VR)	Contraindications (Use Caution)
Patient stability	Stable therapeutic alliance established; patient has insight into condition	Acutely unstable psychiatric condition (new-onset psychosis, mania, active suicidality)
Motivation/openness	Patient is open to technology; motivated to try innovative approaches	Patient exhibits resistance, suspicion, scepticism, or distress toward technology
Diagnosis/target	Anxiety disorders, PTSD, OCD, SUDs, eating disorders, ASD, depression and psychotic disorders (stable phase)	Active psychosis without insight; severe dissociative symptoms
Physical health	No history of seizures; no severe vestibular dysfunction	Epilepsy or seizure risk; severe motion sickness; vestibular disorders
Sensory considerations	Normal or correctable vision; tolerance for headset	Severe sensory processing disorders; migraine/headache exacerbation
Practical factors	Clinician has VR training; appropriate equipment available; informed consent obtained	No standardised training completed; the patient cannot give informed consent

As such, a VR environment may not be suitable for patients experiencing certain types of symptoms.

Conclusion

This chapter has highlighted how VR must be conceptualised as a therapeutic tool within an established therapeutic relationship. Clinicians who consider how VR can impact every step of the therapeutic process will be well-prepared and ready to respond to issues that may arise. Failure to consider these topics endangers the patient, the therapeutic relationship and the credibility of the intervention. As we navigate further into the metaverse, VR will add nuance to the traditional elements of psychotherapy and offer new ways to enhance the therapist-patient relationship.

2

Service Delivery

Introduction

VR has tremendous potential to enhance psychotherapy outcomes by creating highly realistic, immersive environments. Despite a growing evidence base for VR-based interventions, many clinicians remain hesitant to embrace VR due to a lack of standardised training, ethical and safety concerns and risks of cybersickness. Before the COVID-19 pandemic, many clinicians were similarly reluctant to embrace telehealth and remote psychotherapy. The pandemic has taught us that rapid, though not seamless, adoption of new technology is possible. The insights gained as clinicians shifted to telehealth and remote psychotherapy can help inform practitioners implementing VR into clinical practice.

Comparison to Telehealth

Technological advances and increasing demand for mental health services have led many mental health practitioners to implement telehealth for psychotherapy. Conducting assessments and psychotherapy over the telephone, through videoconferencing or using online platforms can increase access to effective treatment for many patients, including those in remote locations or for whom disabilities or lack of resources make traveling to service providers difficult.

While the Veterans Administration in the United States was an early implementer of telehealth, before the COVID-19 pandemic, many mental health practitioners remained hesitant to embrace this avenue for psychotherapy service delivery (Godleski et al., 2012; Caver et al., 2020). A survey conducted in 2018 indicated that nearly 60% of clinical psychologists had never used telepsychology (Glueckauf et al., 2018), mainly due to the lack of training in

DOI: 10.1201/b23370-3

clinical, legal and ethical issues related to this emerging technology. Many of their concerns involved issues like uncertainty of reimbursement, accurately assessing and managing patients in crisis when not meeting in person, how best to protect client confidentiality and adhere to Health Insurance Portability and Accountability Act (HIPAA) guidelines and concerns about how telehealth could affect the therapeutic relationship.

When asked to consider using VR to augment psychotherapy, many clinicians report concerns similar to those posed by telehealth. As a result, very few mental health practitioners have implemented VR into clinical practice despite ample research demonstrating its efficacy for treating many mental health concerns in a safe, ethical and cost-effective manner. A survey of 768 mental health providers revealed that only one provider had incorporated VR into clinical practice (Sampaio et al., 2021).

Telehealth and VR require mental health professionals to adopt technology that may be unfamiliar to them. The nuances of using videoconferencing platforms like Skype for psychotherapy were unfamiliar to many clinicians before the COVID-19 pandemic. However, while the rapid shift to remote therapy was not seamless, it demonstrated that quickly learning new technology is possible for practitioners. Similarly, many clinicians are open to integrating VR into their repertoire but have noted the importance of standardised training for handling patient crises, confidentiality and safety. Currently, there is a push for mental health training programs to develop standardised training protocols for implementing VR into clinical practice.

Though there are similarities between telehealth and VR, VR poses some unique challenges. The headsets required for VR place a physical barrier between the patient and therapist, regardless of whether therapy is in-person or remote. Therapists are skilled at observing changes in patients' affect, eye contact and other non-verbal behaviours that may be masked by VR headsets. Immersive VR environments in which patients and therapists interact as avatars face similar challenges. Despite advancements in technology, VR avatars do not manifest the same facial expressions, gestures and non-verbal behaviours that therapists identify as important cues to their patients' internal experiences.

While incorporating biofeedback sensors into VR can partially address this challenge, further research is necessary to understand how the psychotherapeutic process is altered by patients (and possibly therapists) wearing headsets. Clinicians who have successfully implemented VR into their clinical practice emphasise the importance of developing and maintaining a strong therapeutic alliance before initiating VR interventions. The metaverse represents the endpoint in the progressive adoption of immersive technologies in mental health care (see Figure 2.1). This means that until it is fully accessible, much of what occurs between patients and therapists will continue to be "face-to-face," regardless of whether therapy is in-person or remote.

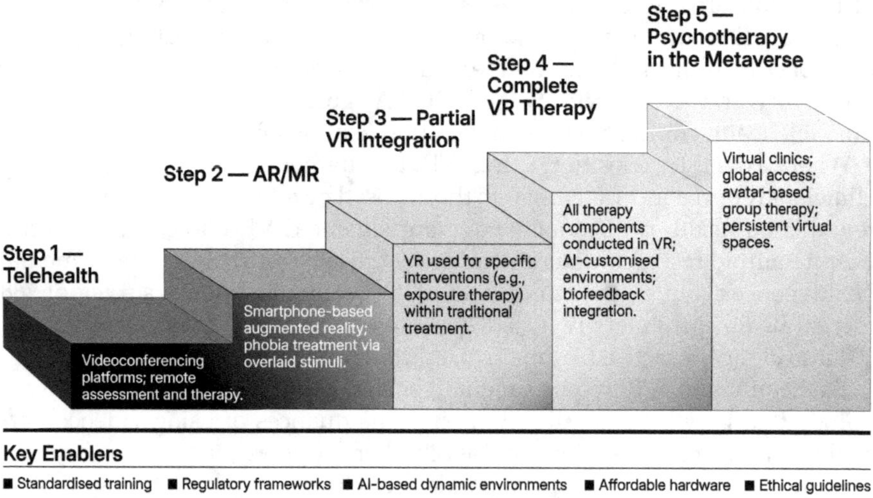

FIGURE 2.1
Adoption readiness model: From telehealth to VR to metaverse.

In-Person versus Remote Delivery

Traditional Psychotherapy

Public health measures and widespread shutdowns during the early part of the COVID-19 global pandemic catalysed a rapid transition from in-person to remote mental health services. A survey of 768 mental health professionals in the United States revealed that while only 39% used telepsychology before COVID-19, 98% implemented it in response to the pandemic (Sampaio et al., 2021). A similar study revealed a 12-fold increase in the use of telepsychology by licensed clinical psychologists, with 85% of clinicians implementing online therapy during the pandemic and 67% conducting their clinical work solely through online platforms (Pierce et al., 2020).

The COVID-19 pandemic prompted regulatory changes that eased the transition to remote therapy for many service providers. Medicare and veterans hospitals allowed therapists to bill and be reimbursed for remote services at the same rate as in-person care. Additionally, the United States Department of Health relaxed HIPAA regulations so that apps like Skype, FaceTime and Zoom could be used to provide remote psychotherapy. Some states eased licensing regulations to allow therapists from other states to treat patients within their state via telepsychology (Pierce et al., 2020; Sampaio et al., 2021).

As the COVID-19 pandemic evolved, many mental health practitioners continued to use telehealth, either exclusively or for patients who felt more comfortable not meeting in person. This increase in implementation made it possible to conduct large-scale investigations comparing remote therapy to in-person care. In a review of 22 randomised controlled trials (RCTs) investigating the efficacy of telehealth (provided via phone or videoconferencing) compared to in-person psychotherapy for PTSD, depression or mixed diagnoses, Bellanti and colleagues (2022) reported that the majority of studies revealed no significant differences in outcome, patient satisfaction with care or quality of the therapeutic alliance. Similarly, a meta-analysis of RCTs comparing telehealth to in-person treatment for depression found comparable effectiveness and similar attrition rates (Giovanetti et al., 2022). Another meta-analysis of RCTs found that telehealth produced clinically meaningful and large reductions in symptoms and reported no significant differences between in-person and telehealth in terms of outcomes at post-treatment and follow-up (Lin et al., 2022).

Aside from ethical, legal and security concerns associated with telehealth, many mental health practitioners are hesitant to embrace remote or online therapy due to the potential impact of technology on the therapeutic alliance. The therapeutic alliance, or the working relationship between patients and their therapists, is an empirically supported relationship factor that is well-established as a predictor of symptom improvement, retention and outcome in psychotherapy (e.g., Falkenström et al., 2013; Flückiger et al., 2018; Norcross, 2001; Weck et al., 2015).

While research investigating the impact of remote therapy on the therapeutic alliance is still emerging, the results of early studies demonstrate that a strong therapeutic alliance can be developed and maintained during remote therapy. In a study of electronic therapy (or "e-therapy") conducted via email, video conferencing, VR and chat technology, Sucala and colleagues (2012) found that the therapeutic alliance in e-therapy was equivalent to in-person therapy and that, similar to in-person therapy, there was an association between therapeutic alliance and e-therapy outcome. A survey of 141 therapists who transitioned to video therapy during the pandemic revealed that the majority of therapists reported maintaining strong therapeutic relationships with their patients despite this shift (Aafjes-van Doorn et al., 2021). Similarly, a non-inferiority study comparing 479 patients receiving teletherapy during the COVID-19 pandemic to 479 patients receiving in-person therapy before the pandemic found that the therapeutic alliance and clinical outcomes for teletherapy were not inferior to those associated with in-person therapy (Davis et al., 2023).

Another study undertaken in Germany of 189 patients and 57 practitioners who switched to online CBT during the COVID-19 lockdowns showed that while patients reported a comparable therapeutic alliance, therapists reported advantages for in-person therapy (Leuchtenberg et al., 2022). Patients and therapists in this study stated that in-person therapy has some advantages in terms of the content covered in therapy, but that they appreciated the flexibility of online therapy. Over 50% of patients in this study reported a preference for a combination of in-person and online services. This study is likely to reflect the experiences of many by showing that both patients and therapists recognise the advantages and disadvantages of remote psychotherapy service provision.

VR Psychotherapy

The number of mental health practitioners who have integrated VR-based interventions into clinical practice remains low, which means that far fewer have used VR for remote psychotherapy. At the present time, this makes large-scale efficacy studies impossible. However, the results of several smaller studies investigating the utility of VR for remote psychotherapy are encouraging.

One study compared in-person virtual reality exposure therapy (VRET) to remote VRET for acrophobia (fear of heights). Participants in this study completed three remote VRET sessions followed by three in-person sessions (Levy et al., 2016). This study revealed no significant differences in anxiety, presence, or working alliance between remote and in-person VRET. Similarly, Cherestal and colleagues (2021) compared the effectiveness of remote VRET to in-person VRET for 17 patients with aviophobia (fear of flying). Patients in both conditions completed eight hours of intensive VRET, and both groups experienced significant reductions in flight-related anxiety. No significant differences emerged between groups on anxiety or treatment completion rates.

Matsangidou and colleagues (2020) tested the feasibility of using a remote VR system in which patients and therapists are simultaneously immersed in a mutual VR environment for the treatment of eating disorders. This feasibility study did not evaluate the efficacy of an intervention but studied the impact of the shared virtual environment on females at high risk for developing an eating disorder. Previous studies have shown that close relationships can be formed among users within virtual spaces, so these researchers were interested in exploring this possibility for eating disorder treatment (Henderson and Gilding, 2004; Utz, 2000). All seven therapists and 11 of the 14 participants described experiencing a sense of trust and security within the virtual world, and most participants stated that they liked that their therapists had never seen their physical bodies. Participants also reported experiencing high levels of presence and anxiety while immersed in the virtual environment. The researchers concluded that the system had been "providing patients with an anonymous, non-threatening and non-judgmental platform to communicate their inner thoughts and feelings," thus capturing the trust and security built within the therapeutic dyad (Matsangidou et al., 2020, p. 333).

Some studies have evaluated the utility of remote, self-led VRET in which no therapist is present. For example, Kim and colleagues (2017) investigated the efficacy of a mobile VR app for treating social anxiety disorder (SAD). Twenty-two patients with SAD and 30 age- and sex-matched controls completed eight self-training sessions over two weeks. Self-reported social anxiety decreased in both groups, but the clinical group showed larger reductions in anxiety. Additionally, the app demonstrated that participants significantly improved in total speech length, voice-time ratio and self-ratings of anxiety and confidence during their speech performances. This is important because it shows that VR self-training can not only reduce anxiety but also lead to skill improvement and more adaptive behaviour.

Another study investigated an automated VR cognitive intervention for fear of heights (Freeman et al., 2018). In this program, a virtual coach provided psychoeducation on fear and anxiety before guiding participants through evaluating the accuracy of their fears, identifying and challenging safety behaviours and encouraging them to resist avoiding challenging situations. Of 100 participants, 49 were randomly assigned to the VR intervention, while 51 were assigned to treatment as usual. The automated VR intervention was shown to significantly reduce fear of heights; these improvements were maintained at a 4-week follow-up.

Lindner and colleagues (2019) evaluated the utility of a one-session therapist-led VRET for public speaking anxiety, followed by a 4-week online program promoting real-world exposure experiences. Compared to a waitlist control group, the therapist-led VRET plus 4-week online program resulted in significant and clinically meaningful reductions in anxiety. The waitlist control group was subsequently given access to the one-session VRET (remotely) and the 4-week online treatment program, which also resulted in significant and large treatment effects. For both the therapist-led and self-led groups, reductions in anxiety were maintained or increased at six- and twelve-month follow-ups.

Early studies show that remote VR-based psychotherapy can be safe and effective. It is important to note that the VR platforms used for remote therapy should allow therapists to monitor both the patient's actions within the virtual environment and the patient. There are VR systems that are compatible with telehealth that enable therapists to monitor patients' virtual experiences remotely. These systems provide therapists with a 2D view of patients' activity within the virtual environment.

For safety purposes, it is important to ensure that the platform includes a video connection with patients so that therapists can monitor patients' responses and movements. Many VR-based interventions involve exposure to triggers or distressing situations, and it is imperative that therapists continually monitor patients' distress and emotional state. Additionally, patients tend to move around while navigating virtual environments, so therapists need to observe to minimise risks of bumping into things or falling.

If patients become too overwhelmed or distressed, therapists need to be able to end the virtual experience and support patients as they use coping strategies to lower their distress. Therapists should discuss this candidly with patients as part of the informed consent process before initiating VR interventions and identify coping skills that the patient has used successfully in the past to manage emotional distress. Therapists should confirm that they know patients' locations, contact information and availability of local crisis services. Therapists and patients should also discuss how technological difficulties will be managed before beginning remote VR psychotherapy.

Barriers to Use of VR for Psychotherapy

A survey of 70 mental health experts published in 2013 revealed that out of 45 interventions, "use of virtual reality" was rated as the fourth most likely intervention to increase in use over the next decade (Norcross et al., 2013). While research has consistently supported the utility of VR as a tool to improve psychotherapy, and technological advancements have increased the accessibility and affordability of VR systems, widespread integration of VR into clinical practice has not occurred (Sampaio et al., 2021). As summarised in Table 2.1, issues that have impeded integration include a lack of standardised training, a lack of accessible VR platforms developed for psychotherapy and concerns over cybersickness.

Surveys of mental health professionals have revealed that most believe that training programs, licensing boards and professional organisations need to develop standardised training regarding the clinical, legal and ethical issues related to VR psychotherapy (Glueckauf et al., 2018; Ma et al., 2021; Sampaio et al., 2021; Ventura et al., 2018). This training would help ensure that VR is implemented into clinical practice safely and effectively, so that the promising results demonstrated repeatedly in research can be translated into evidence-based practice. Without such training, many mental health practitioners will remain ill-equipped and unwilling to adopt this technology, which will further limit access to effective interventions.

Another issue slowing the integration of VR into clinical practice is the lack of accessible VR platforms developed specifically for psychotherapy. Most platforms and apps are created by software developers and entrepreneurs who are unfamiliar with empirically supported psychotherapeutic interventions, the needs of mental health patients and the important role that therapists and the therapeutic alliance play in recovery. Fully harnessing the clinical potential of VR will require mental health professionals to work with entrepreneurs and software developers to create VR apps and platforms that can meet the needs of patients and clinicians.

TABLE 2.1

Barriers and solutions – telehealth vs. VR psychotherapy

Barrier	Telehealth Experience	VR Parallel	Lesson for VR Adoption
Lack of training	~60% of psychologists had never used telepsychology (Glueckauf et al., 2018)	Survey of 768 providers: only 1 had used VR clinically (Sampaio et al., 2021)	Standardised VR training curricula needed from licensing boards
Therapeutic alliance concerns	Fear that remote contact would weaken the alliance	Headsets mask facial expressions; avatar interactions lack nuance	Build the alliance before introducing VR; use biofeedback to supplement observation
Privacy/ HIPAA	Security of video platforms; data storage	VR collects physiological and behavioural data beyond video	Develop VR-specific data governance guidelines; encrypt all biofeedback data
Crisis management	Difficulty managing crises remotely	The physical barrier of the headset adds another layer of distance	Establish safety protocol and coping plan before initiating VR; confirm patient location
Technology reluctance	Clinicians unfamiliar with video conferencing	Clinicians unfamiliar with VR hardware/ software	The pandemic proved that rapid technological adoption is achievable when benefits are demonstrated
Regulatory barriers	Licensing restrictions across state lines; reimbursement	No VR-specific billing codes; no VR-specific regulatory framework	Advocate for regulatory recognition of VR-assisted psychotherapy

Finally, concerns over cybersickness also prevent mental health professionals from embracing VR psychotherapy. Cybersickness refers to a type of motion sickness resulting from immersive VR that occurs when the visual inputs received by the brain conflict with the movements of the body. Symptoms of cybersickness include dizziness, nausea, disorientation and vomiting. While cybersickness does occur, it is worth noting that the majority of studies investigating VR-based psychotherapy report low rates of cybersickness. Therapy drop-out rates for VR-based therapies also tend to be equivalent to or lower than traditional forms of psychotherapy, which also supports a low rate of cybersickness (Benbow and Anderson, 2019; Opris et al., 2012). Additionally, as technology advances and VR environments become even more realistic and vivid, rates of cybersickness are likely to decline further.

Conclusion

The integration of VR into psychotherapy presents both challenges and opportunities. While initial reluctance mirrors the early scepticism surrounding telehealth, the pandemic demonstrated that clinicians can rapidly adapt to new technology when the benefits outweigh concerns. Research supports the efficacy of VR-based interventions, yet barriers such as training, ethical considerations and cybersickness continue to hinder widespread implementation. Collaboration between mental health professionals and technology developers will be essential in refining VR applications for clinical use.

Despite these hurdles, VR remains a promising tool that can expand access to mental health care and enhance therapeutic outcomes. However, with this innovation comes a host of ethical dilemmas that must be carefully considered. Issues surrounding patient confidentiality, data security, accessibility and safety in virtual environments are some concerns. As therapists navigate this evolving landscape, they must ensure that ethical guidelines and regulatory standards keep pace with technological advancements.

These ethical considerations merit an in-depth look to address critical questions surrounding privacy in the metaverse, equitable access to VR psychotherapy and the unforeseen consequences of immersing patients in virtual worlds. As we push the boundaries of what is possible in mental health care, we must also confront the responsibilities that come with these advancements.

3

Ethical Considerations

Introduction

With the continuous advancements of technology and the incorporation of these advancements into the therapeutic process, there are many ethical considerations for therapists to keep in mind. These ethical considerations highlight the necessity of thoughtful, ethically sound implementation of VR in psychotherapy. Additionally, these considerations emphasise that VR is best used as a therapeutic tool within the context of an established therapeutic alliance. The primary ethical considerations—confidentiality, affordability, accessibility, safety and unforeseen consequences—are summarised in Table 3.1.

Confidentiality

There are many angles to consider concerning the confidentiality of psychotherapy in the metaverse. One major concern that therapists may have is guaranteeing that what is said in virtual spaces remains private (Hayes, 2022). In some ways, these concerns are similar to the privacy concerns associated with internet-based psychotherapy. However, in addition to ensuring the security of internet networks used for therapy and using encryption software for electronic communication, therapists incorporating VR into their practices must protect the privacy of all data collected by the system. VR systems may potentially collect considerable amounts of sensitive data about patients, including behavioural responses, physiological data and/or personal information.

Although the stigma associated with receiving psychological and psychiatric treatment has decreased over recent decades, the privacy of mental health information remains a valid concern for many patients. Virtual psychotherapeutic interventions have the potential to help people recover from serious

DOI: 10.1201/b23370-4

mental health issues like eating disorders, substance abuse and dependence, suicidality and psychosis. For patients to feel comfortable divulging sensitive information that could threaten their relationships or job security, therapists must safeguard patient privacy in the metaverse.

Some VR systems use biofeedback sensors to collect physiological data, including heart rate, heart rate variability, blood pressure, respiration rate, skin conductance and—potentially with continued technological advances—brain wave patterns. Physiological data collected within the context of virtual psychotherapy must be considered and protected as private health information. If released, this data could threaten employment in certain professions or health care coverage.

These privacy concerns underscore the necessity of taking the appropriate steps to address patient confidentiality and privacy in a VR psychotherapy environment. These steps may include, but are not limited to, utilising secure data storage, ensuring data is anonymous whenever possible and obtaining consent from patients regarding the specific type of data to be collected and how that data will be used. Additionally, protecting patients' privacy requires

TABLE 3.1

Ethical considerations framework for VR psychotherapy

Domain	Key Questions	Risks	Recommended Actions
Confidentiality	What data does the VR system collect? How is it stored? Who has access?	Behavioural, physiological and personal data breaches; employment/insurance discrimination	Secure storage; anonymise data; obtain specific consent for each data type; verify VR company data policies
Affordability	Can the patient afford VR hardware? Are there hidden software costs?	Financial burden on patients; exacerbation of healthcare disparities	Offer smartphone-based options; clarify all costs upfront; advocate for insurance recognition
Accessibility	Can patients with diverse abilities use the system?	Exclusion of patients with visual, hearing, cognitive or physical impairments	Select systems with customisable settings; add haptic/audio accommodations; test with diverse users
Safety	What is the plan for cybersickness, emotional distress or real-time emergencies?	Motion sickness; symptom exacerbation; inability to intervene in a crisis	Screen for seizure/vestibular risk; establish crisis protocol; maintain video monitoring during remote VR
Unforeseen consequences	Could VR reinforce avoidance of reality? Are there long-term risks?	VR dependence; blurring of realities; inhibited therapeutic alliance; symptom exacerbation	Monitor for escapism; customise VR to patient readiness; plan for symptom exacerbation; contribute to long-term research

transparency from VR companies regarding the types of data collected and how that data is stored and used. Mental health professionals implementing VR into clinical practice have an ethical responsibility to inform patients of how confidentiality will be maintained in the metaverse as part of the informed consent process. Additionally, licensing, regulatory and training boards should disseminate guidelines for protecting patient privacy in the metaverse.

Affordability and Accessibility

Affordability and accessibility are important ethical considerations that must be explored before implementing VR into one's psychotherapy practice (Hayes, 2022). This poses the question: can we ensure that everyone who may benefit from VR psychotherapy will have access to it? Currently, only a small number of therapists have incorporated VR into practice, which greatly limits accessibility. Mental health practitioners cannot provide VR psychotherapy without developing competency regarding VR hardware and software, implementing VR psychotherapeutic interventions and VR crisis management. Mental health regulatory boards and educational institutions should develop standardised training protocols to address these training needs. Completion of training protocols should be required for mental health professionals to help increase accessibility to this promising technology.

Even if more mental health professionals become trained in VR psychotherapy, the costs associated with these systems remain an accessibility barrier, particularly for clinicians who plan to use remote VR psychotherapy. Although the price of VR systems has become more affordable, the systems remain financially inaccessible to many. Therapists who submit a claim to a patient's insurance company for a therapy session do not get reimbursed a higher amount for having used VR. Moreover, while most people have a smartphone or tablet with which they can access VR, using these devices to access VR yields a less immersive and potentially less effective VR psychotherapy experience.

Therapists must be mindful of the financial burden VR technology can impose on patients and take reasonable steps to address this burden. The cost of VR technology often does not include the cost of updating the software and maintaining the system. Selecting which psychotherapy-specific VR software will best meet the patients' needs also involves consideration of these additional costs. Therapists need to be aware of how often software updates are expected, whether the cost of these updates is included in the initial purchase or whether there are any other hidden costs associated with the software choice. If not considered, these costs can further exacerbate existing disparities in access to the internet, technological literacy and availability of resources.

Finally, VR psychotherapy should be accessible to individuals with diverse abilities, including physical, sensory and/or cognitive impairments. Therapists and researchers need to identify barriers that limit accessibility to VR for individuals with diverse abilities and work to develop accommodations to increase accessibility for patients of all abilities. For example, VR systems with enhanced audio and tactile/haptic capabilities may be required to generate a strong sense of presence in patients with visual impairments. For these patients, virtual environments must contain sound cues to help patients navigate, like the sound of a door creaking open or audible footsteps.

VR technology has the potential to increase accessibility to effective, evidence-based psychotherapy, particularly for patients in rural areas or those for whom disabilities or mental health concerns would make traditional psychotherapy difficult. By addressing issues of affordability and accessibility, therapists can make psychotherapy in the metaverse more inclusive, equitable and more widely available.

Safety and Emergencies

The physical and emotional safety of clients in a psychotherapy setting is paramount. Incorporating VR into psychotherapeutic treatment introduces additional potential safety concerns. It is important to account for and minimise potential risks of VR in therapy, such as motion sickness, discomfort or other adverse reactions to a VR experience (Nichols and Patel, 2002). Furthermore, real-time emergencies should be considered and planned for by therapists.

Important questions for therapists to consider include: while in the metaverse, will I be able to intervene effectively and quickly? Can the proper authorities be notified promptly, if needed? Therapists must have a plan in place for each patient regarding these issues before using VR in therapy. This plan must be clearly communicated to and understood by patients before engaging in VR. The potential risks involved in VR psychotherapy emphasise the necessity of a well-established and strong therapeutic alliance and safety procedures before initiating VR interventions. Therapists must have a firm grasp of their patients' current psychological functioning, history of suicidality or self-injurious behaviour, ability to manage emotional distress and emergency resources available locally, including an emergency contact.

Unforeseen Consequences

Therapists should also be prepared for potential unforeseen consequences of incorporating VR into their psychotherapy sessions. Potential unforeseen consequences may include, but are not limited to, adverse reactions, an inhibited therapeutic alliance or an exacerbation of symptoms (Hayes, 2022; Lundin et al., 2023). In some cases, an individual may have adverse reactions in VR psychotherapy such as enhanced anxiety, distress or panic during a session. As VR can imitate the presence of and immersion into various situations, an individual may experience a strong emotional reaction in response. Therapists should be prepared to manage such reactions by having protocols in place to ensure proper support and safety measures.

Technology can either improve or hinder psychotherapy, depending on the patient and how they respond to and interact with various levels of technological advances. The therapist's competency in these different media also impacts how the patient responds. For instance, VR psychotherapy can help propel an individual's therapeutic experience to reach goals in therapy that they may not have been able to reach otherwise. On the other hand, some clients may feel disconnected or be unexpectedly less comfortable than anticipated while interacting with their therapist through a virtual environment. As one can imagine, this can have negative consequences on the therapeutic alliance. Consequently, therapists need to maintain rapport and address any challenges that may unexpectedly arise with their clients.

In addition to these potential consequences, psychotherapy in the metaverse can lead to an exacerbation of symptoms in some clients. For example, some VR therapy interventions may unintentionally intensify anxieties or trigger distressing memories. To minimise this as much as possible, therapists should carefully design and customise the VR psychotherapy experience based on the client's readiness and their therapeutic goals. Therapists and patients should also have a plan in place to handle symptom exacerbations if they occur.

VR psychotherapy is still in its earliest phases; as such, there is no long-term data available regarding the safety of this technology. Clinicians must bear in mind that this technology may be associated with lasting negative psychological effects (Bell et al., 2020). Future research should consider the impact of VR on how patients relate to the world and whether the blurring of realities that can occur with VR may negatively impact some patients, like those with psychotic disorders. It is possible that VR can be used as a means of escaping reality, rather than as a therapeutic tool to strengthen adaptive behaviour and improve experiences in the real world. This type of avoidance behaviour needs to be identified and addressed before becoming problematic.

Conclusion

As therapists explore the use of VR, they must navigate complex issues related to patient confidentiality, data security, accessibility and safety. The potential for VR to revolutionise mental health care is vast, but its success depends on thoughtful, ethically sound implementation.

Ensuring privacy in the metaverse, addressing financial and technological barriers and preparing for unforeseen consequences are critical steps in making VR psychotherapy both effective and responsible. Ethical considerations must remain at the forefront as clinicians adapt to this evolving technology, ensuring that it serves to enhance the therapeutic process. As VR psychotherapy continues to develop, practitioners and regulatory bodies must work together to establish clear guidelines, ensuring that innovation aligns with best practices in patient care.

Beyond ethical concerns, the very nature of the metaverse shapes how patients engage with VR-based therapy. Various elements influence not only how individuals present themselves in virtual spaces but also how they experience therapeutic interventions. Just as patients in traditional therapy selectively reveal aspects of themselves, avatars in VR can serve as digital extensions of identity, affecting therapeutic authenticity and engagement. Similarly, presence and immersion can redefine emotional and psychological connections within therapy, potentially enhancing or complicating treatment outcomes.

The next chapter will explore how these core components of the metaverse impact VR psychotherapy, examining their implications for treatment effectiveness and the patient experience.

4

Metaverse Elements

Introduction

Elements of the metaverse, like avatars, presence, immersion, perspectives, generalisability and accessibility, can influence how patients experience VR-based interventions, which can impact the effectiveness of the intervention (Burden and Savin-Baden, 2025). Mostly, these elements are not novel or unique to VR, but VR changes how they are experienced. For example, patients in non-VR therapy may intentionally present only parts of themselves to the therapist, while withholding or limiting the therapist's access to other aspects of their personhood; this is similar to creating an avatar in VR. Similarly, engagement and authenticity may be real-world counterparts to presence and immersion. Generalisability and accessibility are equally relevant to VR-based and traditional interventions. The interdependent nature of these VR elements is summarised in Figure 4.1.

Avatar

An avatar is a digital representation of the user within the virtual environment. This representation can take various forms, ranging from simple shapes to cartoonish representations to highly detailed, lifelike human figures. Avatars serve as the user's identity in the VR world, allowing them to interact with virtual objects, environments and other users. In the context of psychotherapy, avatars can be customised to reflect different aspects of a patient's identity or to help them confront specific issues. For instance, a therapist might use an avatar to represent a patient's younger self to address childhood trauma, or to embody a feared object or scenario to facilitate exposure therapy.

DOI: 10.1201/b23370-5

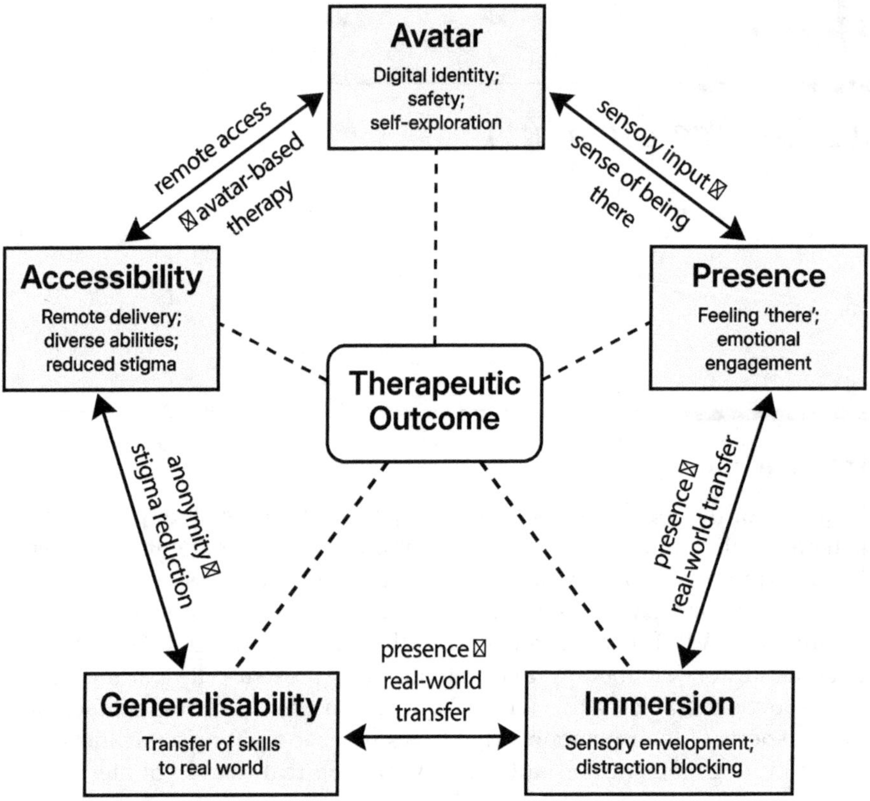

FIGURE 4.1
How metaverse elements interact to influence therapeutic outcomes.

Avatars also play a crucial role in facilitating social interactions within virtual therapeutic groups. Patients can engage with others in a controlled and safe environment, practising social skills and receiving support from peers. This aspect of VR can be particularly beneficial for individuals with social anxiety or other interpersonal difficulties. By interacting through avatars, patients may feel a greater sense of safety and anonymity, which can encourage more open communication and participation in therapy sessions (Matsangidou et al., 2020).

Presence

Presence in VR refers to the psychological state or subjective perception in which the user feels genuinely "there" in the virtual environment. It is the sense of being physically present in a non-physical world, which is crucial for the effectiveness of VR experiences. High levels of presence can enhance the realism of VR therapy, making therapeutic exercises more impactful (Price et al., 2007; Wiederhold and Wiederhold, 2005). For example, a patient undergoing VR exposure therapy for phobias might experience a heightened sense of presence when confronted with virtual representations of their fears, leading to more effective desensitisation.

Achieving presence involves a combination of factors, including realistic graphics, naturalistic interactions and responsive environments. In psychotherapy, maintaining a high level of presence ensures that patients remain engaged and immersed in their therapeutic tasks. For instance, a virtual environment designed to mimic a calming natural setting can help patients practise mindfulness and relaxation techniques more effectively, as the strong sense of presence makes the experience feel more authentic and beneficial.

Immersion

Immersion in VR is the degree to which a user feels enveloped and absorbed by the virtual environment. This is achieved through the use of sensory inputs, such as visual, auditory and haptic feedback, which collectively create a compelling and convincing virtual world. Immersion is crucial in therapeutic settings, as it allows patients to fully engage with the therapeutic content without distractions from the outside world. For example, a fully immersive VR environment for CBT might include simulations with scenes and objects most familiar to the patient, enabling patients to practise coping strategies in a safe and controlled setting.

In a psychotherapeutic context, immersion can be tailored to meet specific therapeutic goals. For instance, a VR program designed to treat PTSD might immerse the patient in a controlled re-experiencing of traumatic events, facilitating exposure and cognitive restructuring. The more immersive the experience, the more likely the patient is to remain focused and emotionally engaged, which can lead to deeper therapeutic insights and more significant progress.

Perspectives

Perspective in VR refers to the viewpoint or angle from which the user experiences the virtual environment. This can include first-person perspectives, where users see the world through the eyes of their avatar, or third-person perspectives, where users view their avatar, therapist and surroundings from an external viewpoint. The choice of perspective can significantly impact the user's experience and the therapeutic outcomes (Riva et al., 2001, 2002). In psychotherapy, different perspectives can be used to facilitate various therapeutic techniques. For instance, a first-person perspective might be employed in exposure therapy to help patients confront their fears directly, while a third-person perspective could be used in role-playing exercises to help patients gain new insights into their behaviour and interactions. Utilising different perspectives can also help in empathy training and social skills development. By experiencing a scenario from another person's point of view, patients can develop a better understanding of others' emotions and reactions. For example, a VR therapy session might involve a patient viewing a conflict from both their own and another person's perspective, fostering empathy and improving their ability to navigate social situations.

Generalisability

Generalisability in the context of VR therapy refers to the extent to which skills and insights gained in the virtual environment can be transferred to real-world situations. This is a critical factor in the effectiveness of VR-based interventions, as the ultimate goal of therapy is to improve the patient's functioning in their everyday life. For instance, a patient who learns to manage anxiety through VR simulations of public speaking should be able to apply those same coping strategies when faced with real-life public speaking situations.

Therapists can enhance the generalisability of VR therapy by designing scenarios that closely mimic real-world challenges and by providing opportunities for repeated practice and incorporating dynamic environments that are as closely related to the real environment as possible. Additionally, the integration of biofeedback and real-time monitoring can help patients gain a deeper understanding of their physiological responses, further aiding in the transfer of skills from the virtual to the real world. By ensuring that therapeutic gains in VR translate to tangible improvements outside of therapy, generalisability maximises the long-term benefits of VR interventions.

Accessibility

Accessibility in VR refers to the ease with which users can engage with virtual environments, regardless of their physical, sensory or cognitive abilities. This encompasses the design of user-friendly interfaces, the availability of assistive technologies and the provision of customisable settings to accommodate various needs. In the realm of psychotherapy, ensuring accessibility is vital to making VR a viable tool for a diverse range of patients. For example, VR systems can be designed with adjustable text sizes, voice commands and haptic feedback to cater to individuals with visual or hearing impairments.

Moreover, VR can significantly increase the accessibility of mental health services by providing remote therapy options. Patients who live in rural areas or have mobility issues can participate in VR therapy sessions from the comfort of their own homes. This flexibility not only broadens the reach of mental health services but also reduces barriers to seeking help, such as stigma and logistical challenges. By prioritising accessibility, VR can democratise access to effective psychotherapeutic interventions, ensuring that more people can benefit from these innovative treatments.

Conclusion

Implementing VR-based interventions requires clinicians to consider therapeutic elements from a new perspective. Because VR is immersive, multisensory and virtual, there is potential for interventions to be profoundly impactful, potentially superseding traditional interventions. For example, because virtual environments can so closely mimic reality and elicit strong emotional responses, skills learned during VR-based interventions may more easily generalise to real-world behaviour. Moreover, as many patients find VR-based interventions preferable to traditional psychotherapy, implementing VR can greatly increase accessibility to evidence-based treatments.

The next chapter will explore the physical components involved in administering VR-based interventions, including the differences between augmented reality, mixed reality and virtual reality. It will also discuss the range of options available for accessing VR technology, from simple smartphone goggles to more expensive headsets.

5

Physical Components

Introduction

This chapter will describe the physical setup required for implementing VR-based interventions. This will include a discussion of how VR differs from augmented reality and mixed reality, comparisons between headsets and phone goggles and descriptions of biofeedback sensors and accessories that can be added to VR systems. The goal is to help clinicians interested in implementing VR-based psychotherapy understand the variety of options available. The different types of systems are summarised in Table 5.1 for a quick comparison.

Augmented/Mixed Reality versus Virtual Reality

Discussions of extended reality (XR) technologies that merge the virtual with the physical can be confusing because terms like virtual reality, mixed reality and augmented reality are often used interchangeably or without clear definitions. Before moving forward, we examine what differentiates these XR technologies.

Virtual reality (VR) refers to a 3D computer-generated environment, into which users are immersed. VR enables users to interact with elements present in the virtual environment, other users and/or avatars. VR is a multisensory experience limited only by the technology on which it relies. The visual and auditory inputs block out the external physical reality.

Basic VR may include only visuospatial and auditory input and be limited to the exploration of a virtual environment, while more advanced VR can include kinaesthetic and haptic inputs and allow naturalistic interaction within the environment, both with other users and/or with elements present

DOI: 10.1201/b23370-6

TABLE 5.1

Descriptions, applications and examples of VR, AR and MR

	Description	Primary Applications	Examples
Virtual Reality (VR)	3D computer-generated environment into which a user is immersed. Users can interact with other users/avatars and virtual elements, but cannot see the physical environment.	Entertainment Education Healthcare Training	Meta Quest 3 HTC VIVE Pro 2 PlayStation VR2 Apple Vision Pro
Augmented Reality (AR)	Overlays virtual elements onto the physical reality via smartphone or tablet. Users can see the physical environment.	Entertainment Marketing	Pokémon Go Instagram filters Apple Vision Pro
Mixed Reality (MR)	A hybrid of VR and AR that combines elements of the physical and virtual environments. Goggles or headsets allow users to "see" virtual elements as if they were a part of the physical reality. Users can interact with and manipulate virtual elements.	Education Training	Microsoft HoloLens Magic Leap One HTC VIVE

in the virtual world. VR is designed to generate a strong sense of presence, such that users perceive themselves to be physically present in the virtual world.

Mixed reality (MR) and augmented reality (AR) are two other XR technologies that, while similar in many ways, have important differences. AR is more limited than MR in that it overlays virtual elements onto a physical reality via a smartphone, tablet or headset passthrough. Popular examples of AR include Pokémon Go, Instagram filters and furniture-fitting apps. AR is often used for entertainment or marketing purposes and is far less interactive than VR or MR.

MR is a hybrid of VR and AR; it combines elements of virtual and physical environments. MR typically requires specialised goggles or glasses that enable you to "see" virtual elements as if they were part of the physical reality in front of you. However, MR hardware differs from VR headsets in that it is completely or partially transparent, allowing the user to see his/her physical surroundings. With MR, users can interact with and manipulate virtual elements as though they were part of the physical world. Microsoft HoloLens, which allows users to manipulate and move holograms, is an example of MR. MR applications are particularly useful for education and training. For example, medical students can use MR programs to rotate, manipulate and interact with holographic hearts.

MR and AR can also be valuable tools used to enhance psychotherapeutic techniques, particularly for anxiety disorders. For example, an intervention could use AR or MR to project phobic objects, like snakes, spiders or vomit into a patient's environment or onto his/her person. Research demonstrating the efficacy of MR/AR technology will be described in the final section of this book, as this type of XR may represent an early step in integrating VR technology into clinical practice. MR/AR is more cost-effective and easier to implement than VR, so clinicians looking to elevate their practice with XR technology may begin with AR/MR. However, as this book is focused on psychotherapy in the metaverse, most of the following sections will focus specifically on VR.

Headset versus Phone Goggles

There are a range of options available for accessing VR technology, from simple smartphone holders to more expensive headsets like the Meta Quest 3 or Apple Vision Pro. Nearly all currently available smartphones have VR capability, regardless of operating system. Smartphone VR systems are created by sliding the smartphone (without a cover) into a goggle-like headset. Google Cardboard was an early example of how simple materials could be used to transform smartphones into VR systems. Google Cardboard headsets are no longer available; however, similar headsets are available for purchase or can be produced fairly easily by users.

Phone goggles require two double-convex lenses, a ring magnet, a ceramic disc magnet, VELCRO® and/or a rubber band to hold the phone in place. The lenses split the phone display into two images (one for each eye) and distort the images to create a stereoscopic or 3D vision that enhances the user's sense of presence. The magnets function as buttons by triggering the magnetometer within the smartphone. Though simple, most smartphone goggles allow motion tracking, stereoscopic rendering and user interaction within immersive virtual environments.

While smartphone goggles make VR accessible to anyone with a smartphone, the VR experience is often of low quality. VR headsets are more expensive but offer significantly improved virtual experiences due to the greater processing power afforded by more advanced software. The cost of the system is a major factor for many therapists in deciding which to select, and the estimated retail prices are compared in Table 5.2. Some VR headsets function as stand-alone devices, while others require tethering to PCs or gaming systems. These headsets vary significantly in terms of available features, intended uses and price. The following list describes some of the most popular currently available VR headsets. This list is not intended to be exhaustive, but to describe the range of options and distinguishing features of available VR headsets.

- Meta Quest 3: This headset is a stand-alone system that can be used for immersive VR experiences or mixed reality. This is one of the more affordable options, with a price of around $485. In addition to its capability for VR and MR, a selling point of this VR headset is the Touch Plus controllers that provide realistic sensations and enable natural interactions. Direct Touch technology allows users to navigate without controllers by using movement sensors to follow hand gestures, allowing users to navigate using only their hands. This system is primarily marketed for gaming, entertainment and collaboration.
- PlayStation VR2: This popular VR headset is designed to work with the PlayStation 5 gaming system and features 3D audio immersion that produces highly realistic soundscapes that adapt to users' position and movement. This headset also creates visually compelling experiences with 4K HDR resolution and eye tracking. Vibrations produced by the headset add a tactile element and the Sense Controller detects placement of fingers even when users are not pressing buttons, which

TABLE 5.2

VR platforms summarising special features and prices

System	Special Features	Estimated Price (USD)
Meta Quest 3	• Touch Plus controllers allow natural interactions with realistic sensations • Direct Touch Technology enables navigation using movement sensors located in the hand controls • Stand-alone system	$485
PlayStation VR2	• 3D audio immersion creates highly realistic soundscapes • 4K resolution and eye tracking • Sense controllers detect finger placement and allow haptic feedback • Tethered to PS5	$600
HTC VIVE Pro2	• Headphones with 3D spatial sound integration • Headset with a 5K resolution display and a wide FOV • Precision movement tracking • Tethered to a gaming PC	$1,199
Apple Vision Pro	• Eye and hand tracking with only a headset • No additional controllers • Navigate apps with hands, eyes and voice • Fitted to a single user	$3,499

allows for haptic feedback and adaptive triggers that sense finger tension. PlayStation VR2 can be purchased for $600. The system is primarily marketed for gaming.

- HTC Vive Pro 2: This VR system requires a gaming PC and includes high-resolution certified headphones with 3D spatial sound integration to produce high-quality soundscapes. The headset has a visually stunning 5K display and a wide field of vision that more naturally simulates human vision and employs precision movement tracking. This system is marketed for gaming, productivity and entertainment. The retail price of this system is $1,199.
- Apple Vision Pro: This stand-alone headset offers ground-breaking eye and hand tracking and requires no additional controllers. This headset is marketed as a "spatial computer" but has both VR and AR capabilities and allows the user to navigate apps with eyes, hands and voice. Unlike the other headsets described, Apple Vision Pro can only be fitted to a single user and works best from a sitting position. The retail price of this headset is $3,499. This system is marketed primarily for productivity and entertainment.

The VR systems described above were mainly created to enhance gaming and entertainment. However, several mental health practitioners have worked with software developers to create specialised VR psychotherapy platforms. These platforms use VR to create realistic, immersive experiences that can be integrated into psychotherapy for a broad range of mental health conditions.

Biofeedback Sensors

Biofeedback sensors, as in Table 5.3, can be incorporated into VR systems and provide valuable, objective measures of patients' physiological reactions during virtual interventions. While clinicians are skilled at observing changes in patients' demeanour, affect, eye contact, facial expressions and other nonverbal cues, objective measurements can supplement clinical observation and facilitate patients' understanding of the connection between mind and body. Additionally, VR headsets block therapists from seeing a large portion of patients' faces, including their eyes, which can hinder clinical observations. The following list describes biofeedback sensors relevant to VR-based psychotherapy (Guillen-Sanz et al., 2024).

- Electroencephalography (EEG) measures electrical activity in the brain via electrodes attached to the scalp. Electrical activity forms characteristic brain wave patterns that reflect mental processes like attention, sleep and relaxation.

- Electromyography (EMG) uses electrodes attached to the skin to measure the electrical activity of a muscle as it contracts. Electrical activity in the muscles can reflect tension, movement and facial expressions, depending on the location of the electrodes.
- Electrocardiogram (ECG) uses sensor pads placed on the chest, lower trunk or wrists to measure aspects of cardiovascular activity like heart rate (HR) and heart rate variability (HRV). HRV reflects the variation in time between heartbeats and provides information about autonomic nervous system function. Low HRV is associated with autonomic arousal (fight or flight response) and vulnerability to stress, while high HRV is indicative of cardiovascular health and stress resilience.
- Electrodermal activity (EDA), also referred to as galvanic skin response, measures the electrical conductivity of the skin and sweat gland activity through sensors placed on the skin. Sensors are placed in areas with a high density of sweat glands, like the hands, feet and neck. These measurements indirectly reflect autonomic nervous system activation, as stress and fear trigger the sweat glands to produce sweat.
- Respiration rate and depth can be measured by placing belts or movement sensors around the abdomen or chest. These sensors measure

TABLE 5.3

Summary of device, type of data collected, sensor type and information provided

Device	Data Collected	Sensor Type	Information Provided
Electroencephalography (EEG)	Electrical activity in the brain	Electrodes placed on the scalp	Attention Sleep Relaxation
Electromyography (EMG)	Electrical activity during muscle contraction	Electrodes placed on the skin	Tension Movement Facial Expressions
Electrocardiogram (ECG)	Heart rate Heart rate variability	Sensor pads on the chest, lower trunk and wrists	Stress Fear Relaxation
Electrodermal Activity (galvanic skin response)	Electrical conductance of the skin Sweat gland activity	Sensors on hands, feet and neck	Stress Fear Relaxation
Respiration	Respiration rate Respiration depth	Belts or movement sensors on the abdomen/chest	Stress Fear Relaxation
Eye Tracking	Pupil size Eye movement	Sensors inside goggles/headset	Attention Gaze Stress Fear Relaxation

the rate and amplitude of bodily movement associated with respiration. Frequent, shallow breaths are associated with stress or physiological arousal, whereas slower, deeper respiration signals relaxation.

- Eye-tracking devices assess pupil size and movement and are used to determine gaze and emotional state. Location of gaze is used to determine the focus of attention, while increases in pupil size can reflect sympathetic nervous system activation, as pupils dilate to let more light into the eye and enhance vision during stress.

There are many options available for incorporating biofeedback into VR systems. However, adding these components to existing VR systems often results in a bulky and cumbersome experience for the user. These components can be expensive, so adding several biofeedback sensors greatly increases the operating cost of implementing VR into clinical practice. Additionally, consolidating data collected from multiple biofeedback devices simultaneously exceeds the capability of many VR software programs. These challenges limit the number of biofeedback devices that can be incorporated into clinical practice, which can give an incomplete or misleading picture of patients' experiences.

To address these challenges, Gnacek and colleagues (2022) developed emteqPRO as an all-in-one headset insert specifically designed to provide biofeedback data relevant to psychological research and treatment. The emteqPRO can be inserted into several existing VR headsets and is unique in that it contains integrated sensors that detect patients' facial expressions via EMG. Additional sensors included in the insert measure gaze, pupil size, heart rate and heart rate variability. The emteqPRO's software aggregates data from these sensors to generate comprehensive and accurate reports on patients' emotional states during VR experiences. This is one example of how biofeedback can be successfully implemented into VR psychotherapy to provide valuable information that can be used to inform, modify and enhance psychotherapeutic interventions.

Accessories

In addition to biofeedback sensors, accessories can be added to VR systems to enhance the users' experience and the clinical utility of VR psychotherapy. The following list is not exhaustive but contains the accessories most relevant to VR psychotherapy.

- Hand-held controllers allow users to touch, pick up or interact with objects in a virtual environment.
- Specialised devices like steering wheels and pedals may be added for exposure therapy to address driving phobias or PTSD.
- Haptic feedback accessories like haptic gloves provide tactile input to increase the realism of touching and interacting with virtual objects.

Haptic vests, arm bands and leg and foot bands can extend tactile sensations to various body parts.

- Vibration platforms can be used to create kinaesthetic sensations for simulations involving airplanes, explosions or natural disasters. These sensations can also be generated through some haptic feedback accessories.
- Olfactory accessories that generate scents like alcohol, foods or gunpowder can augment exposures for substance abuse treatment, eating disorders and combat-related PTSD.

Other important VR accessories are used to protect VR equipment and promote a comfortable experience for users. These include VR cases, lens covers for headsets, grip covers with straps to prevent hand controllers from being thrown or dropped during activity, external battery packs that prolong battery life to lengthen user experiences and headset covers to prevent skin irritation and wick sweat away from the skin. Including biofeedback devices and other accessories can help bridge the gap until psychotherapy-specific software is more widely available.

Conclusion

This chapter described the physical components and accessories that can be used to implement VR-based interventions into clinical practice. Understanding the range of options available can help clinicians determine how to integrate VR into their practice. Clinicians must consider the advantages and disadvantages of augmented reality, mixed reality and virtual reality to determine which extended reality is best suited for their practice. Clinicians must also consider the expense and quality of smartphone goggles and VR headsets to determine which hardware will best serve their patients' needs.

Additionally, clinicians can augment VR systems with biofeedback sensors and accessories to enhance patients' experiences and the clinical utility of VR-based interventions. Clinicians must consider the financial resources and technical skill level of both themselves and their patients when determining which components and accessories to include in their practice. The next chapter will describe the virtual environments that patients are immersed in during VR-based interventions and will include a discussion of the advantages and disadvantages of video-based and computer-based virtual environments.

6

Virtual Environments

Introduction

Virtual environment (VE) refers to the multisensory, simulated environment into which the patient is immersed during VR-based interventions. The more realistic and multisensory the VE, the more the patients feel a strong sense of presence and immersion, which can enhance the effectiveness of the intervention. The two main types of VEs used by mental health practitioners are video-based VEs and computer-generated VEs.

The following sections, summarised in Table 6.1, will describe these VEs and address the advantages and disadvantages of each to help clinicians determine the best VEs for their patients. Making this decision requires consideration of many factors, including the financial resources and technical skill level of clinicians and patients and the psychological conditions commonly treated by a particular clinician.

Video-Based Virtual Environment

Omnidirectional, spherical cameras capture a 360° view of objects, experiences and locations. When viewed through a head-mounted device, the footage transforms into a highly realistic immersive experience. Using 360° video to create VEs has several advantages over using computer-based VEs. Video-based VEs look more realistic than those that are computer-generated because they use actual footage of real-world phenomena. Moreover, video-based VEs are considerably less expensive to produce and can be created without high-level programming skills. Clinicians can create these environments themselves, using footage they have shot or accessing footage freely available on the internet. These advantages make for easier implementation of VR into clinical practice.

DOI: 10.1201/b23370-7

Although video-based VEs are less expensive and more realistic, they do not allow for the same level of interaction within the VE as computer-generated VEs. Video-based VEs can be explored by users because motion trackers shift the view depending on head position and movement; however, users cannot touch, pick up or interact with any elements in the environment. Lack of interaction within the VE limits the applicability of this technology for some psychotherapeutic interventions, although there are still many types of exposures that can be enhanced by using video-based VEs. For example, immersion into video-based VEs of large crowds, subway cars or other crowded venues can be used in exposure therapy for panic disorder with agoraphobia.

Another limitation of video-based VEs is that they cannot be customised or manipulated. This limits the range of patient fears or triggers that can be addressed by VR-based interventions by making it impossible to create individually tailored exposures for specific patient needs. Interventions for more complicated and idiosyncratic disorders like obsessive-compulsive disorder or eating disorders may require more intricate computer-generated VEs.

Additionally, patients' experiences cannot be incrementally graduated using video-based VEs. Exposure therapy proceeds gradually; patients begin by mastering exposures to minimally or moderately distressing stimuli before moving on to highly distressing stimuli. This gradation is not possible with video-based VEs. Instead, patients would have to begin with exposure to less realistic or even cartoonish stimuli before working up to exposure to the realistic images produced by these VEs.

Despite these limitations, research has shown that video-based VEs can be used effectively to reduce phobias and depression. Holmberg and colleagues (2020) found that video-based VEs elicited anxiety and presence in nine patients with social anxiety disorder. Control participants reported no increase in anxiety. Upon completion of the study, patients reported that the videos felt authentic and supported using these VEs as initial treatment steps before engaging in real-world exposures.

In another study, virtual reality exposure therapy (VRET) for public speaking anxiety (PSA) was evaluated in 51 participants who were randomly assigned to either a video-based VE containing an audience, a video-based VE of an empty room or no treatment (Reeves et al., 2021). Significant reductions in PSA were observed for participants who completed four sessions of VRET with audience stimuli, and these reductions were maintained at a 10-week follow-up.

Lundin and colleagues (2021) investigated the efficacy of video-based VEs for 12 patients with panic disorder with agoraphobia (PDA). The VEs used in this study contained stimuli that many patients with PDA find triggering, including subways, walking tunnels, busy train stations, elevators, auditoriums and tall bridges. Following 10–12 weeks of treatment, patients in this study reported significant improvements in PDA-related symptoms, and improvements were maintained at a 6-month follow-up. Additionally, all patients completed treatment and reported high satisfaction with it. This is impressive given that many patients with panic disorder and agoraphobia find exposure therapy to be too distressing to complete.

One study evaluated whether video-based VEs could be used effectively for behavioural activation to address depression in a patient during the COVID-19 lockdowns (Paul et al., 2020). In this case study, a therapist selected 360° videos available on YouTube to correspond with items on the Pleasant Events Schedule, an assessment used to supplement behavioural activation. The VEs in this study contained stimuli related to animals, sports, arts, travel and outdoor activities. Engagement with these VEs was associated with a clinically significant reduction in depression symptoms, which the patient attributed to both the VEs and increased engagement in real-world activities. This demonstrates that the effects of virtual behavioural activation generalised to real-world behaviour.

Ionescu and colleagues (2021) noted the dramatic contrast between the potential of VR to enhance psychotherapy and its actual uptake into clinical practice. These researchers identify that the high cost and programming skills necessary for computer-generated VEs are prohibitive for many clinicians and speculate that video-based VR may be one way to increase integration of VR into clinical practice. They conducted a systematic review of studies that have used video-based VEs for a broad range of mental health conditions and reported medium to large effect sizes for interventions targeting anxiety. They also found that video-based VEs can effectively improve mood and that these interventions are associated with few negative effects. Importantly, they found that most of the VEs used in these studies were created by the mental health professionals using them, which underscores the ease of implementation of this type of VR technology.

Computer-Based Environments

Computer-generated VEs allow users to explore and interact within digitally simulated realities of the physical world. Despite technological advances, computer-generated VEs provide less realistic, lower-resolution renderings than video-based VEs. Creation of computer-generated VEs requires a high level of programming skills, which means that this type of VR involves a significant financial investment for implementation into clinical practice.

Computer-generated VEs increase the range of psychological conditions that can be addressed using VR technology. Video-based VEs are limited only to experiences or environments that can be captured in real-time. On the other hand, computer-generated VEs can allow users to interact in environments that are otherwise impossible, inaccessible or unsafe. For example, VR-based interventions for eating disorders enable patients to navigate painful past experiences. VR-based exposure therapy for OCD can safely expose patients to filthy bathrooms or, for patients with PTSD, to combat environments or natural disasters.

Computer-generated VEs are customisable, which means that they can be tailored to address the specific fears, triggers or issues presented by patients. Therapists can customise the VE to simulate past experiences, traumas or specific feared situations so that therapy can be tailored to each patient. Additionally, elements within the VE can be simplified or amplified, which allows for gradation within exposure therapy. For example, a therapist can modify parameters (e.g., size, gender or composition) of a virtual audience to decrease or increase a patient's anxiety during public speaking exposure.

Customisable computer-generated VEs can enhance the learning of new skills within a realistic environment free from risks that may be present in the real world. Patients in substance abuse treatment can practise refusal skills while immersed in bars, restaurants or parties without the risks presented by the presence of actual intoxicating substances or unpredictable behaviour of others who may be intoxicated. Patients with persecutory delusions can practise routine social interactions without risk of being taunted or treated poorly.

There is ample evidence demonstrating the efficacy of VR-based interventions using computer-generated VEs. Part two of this book will describe these studies and explore how this technology can enhance outcomes for a broad range of mental health conditions.

How to Compare Different Platforms

Clinicians who have decided to integrate VR into their clinical practice must determine which VR platform is the best option for the patients they treat. In addition to choosing the optimal hardware for their practice, clinicians must select from a variety of commercially available VR platforms that have been designed specifically for psychotherapy.

Choosing the best hardware for a clinical practice requires consideration of the conditions most frequently treated within the practice and the demographic of the patients. For clinicians who primarily treat phobias, social anxiety disorder or mood disorders, video-based VR may be sufficient. This type of VR can be used effectively with patients' smartphones and may only require the purchase of VR goggles for inserting smartphones. Clinicians who are primarily treating more complex disorders like OCD, PTSD, eating disorders or substance use disorders may need more advanced VR headsets, like the Meta Quest 3 or HTC Vive, for computer-generated virtual environments.

TABLE 6.1

VE type, description, advantages and disadvantages

Type of VE	Description	Advantages	Disadvantages
Video-based	Omnidirectional spherical camera captures 360° view of objects, experiences and locations	• More realistic • Less expensive • Easier to create • Patients can explore the VE • It does not require high-level programming skills • Easier implementation into clinical practice • Demonstrated efficacy in treating phobias and depression	• Users cannot interact with the VE • VE cannot be customised or manipulated • Patients' experiences cannot be incrementally graduated
Computer-generated	Created via computer programming software	• Allows patients to interact with and explore the VE • Increases the range of psychological conditions that can be addressed with VR • Allows patients to interact in environments that are impossible, inaccessible or unsafe • Can be customised to address specific patients' needs • Patients' experiences can be incrementally graduated • Patients can practise skills in a realistic VE	• Less realistic • More expensive • Requires high-level programming skills • More difficult to implement into clinical practice

Choice of hardware will also depend on whether clinicians intend to use VR-based interventions in-office or via remote therapy. Clinicians using VR for remote psychotherapy must verify that the hardware they choose is compatible with software programs that allow them to monitor patients' activities within virtual environments, while simultaneously monitoring patients' reactions and safety via videoconferencing. Clinicians using VR remotely must also consider the financial resources of their patients; nearly all patients have access to smartphones, but purchasing expensive head-mounted devices may not be feasible.

Clinicians must also decide whether to use biofeedback devices or other accessories with their VR-based interventions. Biofeedback inserts like the emteqPRO described previously are designed to work with many VR headsets, but not with smartphone goggles. Similarly, there may be additional accessories like haptic gloves or vibrating platforms that can enhance virtual environments. These accessories are typically compatible with more advanced head-mounted devices.

Once clinicians have selected the equipment that will best meet their patients' needs, they must determine which software package is compatible with the hardware they have selected and contains the psychotherapy content necessary to address these needs. Again, this decision may vary depending on whether clinicians intend to use VR-based interventions in-person or via remote psychotherapy. Clinicians conducting VR-based remote therapy need to carefully consider the demographics of their patients. Do most of their patients have the financial resources to allow for more high-tech headsets like the Vive Pro or Meta Quest, or does the VR platform need to be compatible with VR that uses smartphone goggles?

Clinicians using remote VR-based interventions must check that the software package includes video monitoring of the client's experiences within the virtual environment with simultaneous videoconferencing with the patient. This ensures that therapists can see what the patient is doing within the virtual environment, while monitoring physical safety (i.e., reducing risk of tripping or running into furniture) and reactions to the virtual interventions. For remote VR-based therapy, patients will need to have two devices; patients cannot use their smartphones for videoconferencing while immersed in the virtual environment.

Clinicians must also consider the range of mental health conditions that they will be addressing with VR-based interventions. The content of some software packages can be used in a broad range of interventions, while others are more targeted and specific. Some software packages are more comprehensive and include psychoeducation/instructional content as well as exposures and relaxation/reward environments, while others may contain only content used for exposure therapy. Some packages also offer training for clinicians or technical support.

Considering the demographics of the patients can also inform decision-making regarding which software package will work best for a particular clinician. If patients have vision or hearing issues, they may require software with accommodations to increase accessibility. Are there any language or cultural barriers that may impede the efficacy of VR with the patient population? Is there a need for diverse VR content, including avatars that represent patients of various ethnicities, skin colours and sexual orientations? If the software contains relaxation or reward environments, is the content of these environments likely to appeal to most patients treated within the practice?

Furthermore, it is important for clinicians to have a clear picture of the costs involved in adding VR to clinical practice. Prior to purchase or subscription, clinicians should understand whether there are monthly or periodic costs associated with the software package, whether there is usage-based pricing or whether the initial cost covers full usage. Clinicians should also ask how software updates or new versions are rolled out and the frequency with which these may occur. Are updates and new versions included in the initial costs, or will there be separate charges for each? Clinicians can also inquire about whether any peer-reviewed publications have demonstrated the clinical efficacy of a particular software or whether the company can provide contact information for other therapists who have used the psychotherapy VR software.

Conclusion

Selecting the right hardware and software for VR-based interventions involves careful consideration of many factors. Clinicians must consider the costs of VR equipment and the technical expertise required to use it. The costs and benefits of each choice must be weighed to decide which will best serve their patient population. Additional considerations include whether they plan to use VR-based interventions in-person or remotely, compatibility between hardware and software and the specific psychological conditions treated. For instance, a clinician treating phobias and anxiety disorders might opt for a simpler, video-based VR setup that can be used with a patient's smartphone. In contrast, a clinician working with patients with PTSD or complex trauma might require a more sophisticated, computer-generated VR environment with advanced features like haptic feedback.

Clinicians should research the costs associated with the software package, including monthly fees, usage-based pricing and the frequency of software updates and new versions. They should also review published research on the software's clinical efficacy and seek out reviews from other therapists who have used it. By carefully considering all these factors, clinicians can make informed decisions about how to integrate VR into their practice in a way that will best meet the needs of their patients.

Part 2

Applied Models for VR Psychotherapy

Introduction

Virtual reality (VR) is a powerful tool to enhance evidence-based psychotherapy for a broad range of mental health conditions. In the context of an established therapeutic relationship between an engaged patient and a competent therapist, VR can bolster therapeutic interventions by enhancing patient outcomes, improving cost-effectiveness and increasing patients' motivation and willingness to fully engage in the treatment process (Powers and Emmelkamp, 2008; Meyerbröker et al., 2022).

This section explores the application of VR technology to three broad areas within the cognitive-behavioural framework. Cognitive behavioural therapy (CBT) is the modality of psychotherapy that has been most extensively researched with VR. Many of the same themes are repeated across diagnoses, which is why Part 2 has been divided into the core elements of CBT.

The first chapter in this section addresses how VR enhances *cue/sensory desensitisation* via exposure therapy and describes the applications for anxiety disorders, PTSD, OCD, substance use disorders and eating disorders. The second chapter discusses VR's utility for *cognitive training*, including distraction techniques to shift attention, cognitive restructuring, challenging and replacing negative or distorted beliefs and memories and improving executive functioning. Applications for pain management, chronic pain, eating disorders, psychotic disorders and depression are also presented in

DOI: 10.1201/b23370-8

TABLE 7.1

Summary of Part 2 content

Chapter	Intervention	Condition Addressed
Cue/Sensory Desensitisation	Exposure therapy	Anxiety disorders PTSD OCD Substance use disorders Eating disorders
Cognitive Training	Distraction techniques Cognitive Restructuring Executive Functioning Training	Chronic and acute pain Eating Disorders Psychotic Disorders Depression
Skills Training	Social Skills Training Life Skills Training Refusal Skills Training Craving Management Emotion Regulation	Autism spectrum disorder Psychotic disorders Substance use disorders Disorders involving emotional dysregulation

this section. The final chapter describes VR's potential for enhancing various types of *skills training* included in CBT. Applications for social skills training for individuals with autism spectrum disorders or psychotic disorders, refusal and craving management skills for addiction and emotion regulation skills to improve well-being are also described. Table 7.1 summarises the interventions and conditions addressed in each chapter of this section.

7

Cue/Sensory Desensitisation

Introduction

Many psychological disorders are characterised by excessive fear or distress triggered by specific objects or situations, including anxiety disorders, PTSD, OCD, substance use disorders and eating disorders. While these disorders differ in important ways, the underlying pathology common to each is a destructive cycle in which a cue triggers a cascade of distressing or maladaptive thoughts, emotions and behaviours. Cues take many forms, depending on the specific disorder in question. Cues can be *objects*, like snakes, fireworks, an unflushed toilet or a billboard advertising whiskey, or *bodily sensations* like light-headedness, dizziness or increased heart rate. A cue can be an *automatic thought* that occurs without notice, like thinking that everyone is judging you, or an intrusive image or memory that triggers intense distress. *Situations* like being in a crowd, waiting in line or eating at a restaurant can also be cues.

Regardless of their form, the brain reacts to cues with alarm and triggers several physiological reactions in the body, like increased heart rate, blood pressure and respiration rate. In the face of real danger, these reactions are adaptive because they ensure that the muscles needed for fighting or fleeing are well supplied with oxygen and nutrients. But the brain is not well equipped to distinguish real danger from false alarms, which sets the stage for the development of maladaptive patterns of unhealthy thoughts, emotions and behaviours.

As these anxious or distorted thoughts and emotions feed on each other, the level of anxiety and distress escalates and becomes overwhelming. High levels of emotional distress cause people to behave in maladaptive ways, like avoidance, performing rituals, engaging in substance use or bingeing/purging. Though these behavioural manifestations look very different, the purpose of each is to minimise anxiety and distress.

For example, a patient with a phobia of heights may experience light-headedness when looking out of a top-floor window of a skyscraper. He misinterprets light-headedness as an indication that something bad will happen or that he is in danger, which further increases his anxiety and causes him to avoid heights, which prevents him from applying for his dream

DOI: 10.1201/b23370-9

job because his office would be high in a skyscraper. Distressing, intrusive thoughts that trigger compulsive handwashing in a patient with OCD may cause the patient to refuse to use public restrooms; this avoidance could make working outside the home or engaging in social activities impossible.

As demonstrated in Figure 7.1, many of the behaviours associated with these disorders involve *avoidance*. Like cues, avoidance manifests in many ways. These disorders leave many people unable to sustain relationships or work or find joy in life because the need to avoid social situations, intense emotions, trauma triggers, food-related events and other meaningful activities increases. An escape or avoidance reaction is a natural human tendency to an anxiety-provoking situation. CBT is the empirically supported treatment for anxiety disorders (Butler et al., 2006; Deacon and Abramowitz, 2004; Nathan and Gorman, 2002) and works by interrupting this cycle. Therapists help patients understand the relationships between their thoughts, feelings and behaviours. In CBT, therapists and patients collaborate to identify specific

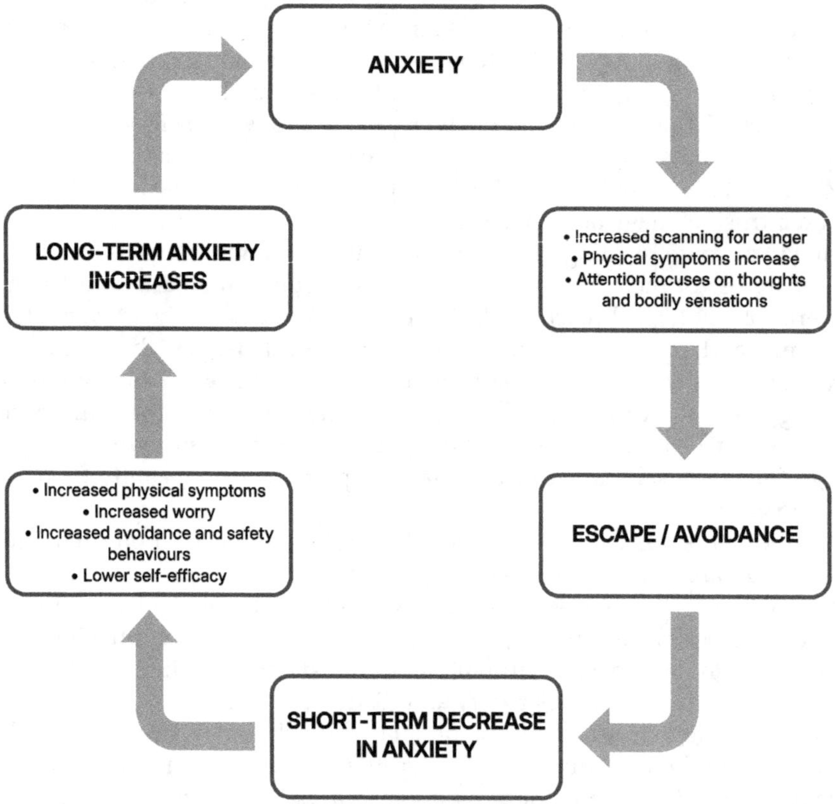

FIGURE 7.1
The anxiety-avoidance cycle perpetuates anxiety.

thoughts and beliefs that are triggered by cues, recognise the emotions these thoughts and beliefs elicit and observe how these thoughts and emotions result in unhealthy or self-defeating behaviours. As therapy progresses, patients learn to challenge their thought patterns or faulty beliefs, manage emotional distress and engage meaningfully with others through social events, work and leisure activities.

The cognitive component of CBT involves teaching clients to recognise the distortions and errors in thinking that exacerbate fear, anxiety and distress and to identify how these thoughts negatively influence their emotions and behaviour, as shown in Figure 7.2. Therapists teach patients to challenge these thoughts by finding evidence to confirm or disconfirm them. Patients practise replacing these thoughts with those that are more realistic, flexible and adaptive. They also track how changing these thoughts improves their mood and leads to more adaptive behaviour. This will be discussed more fully in the next section.

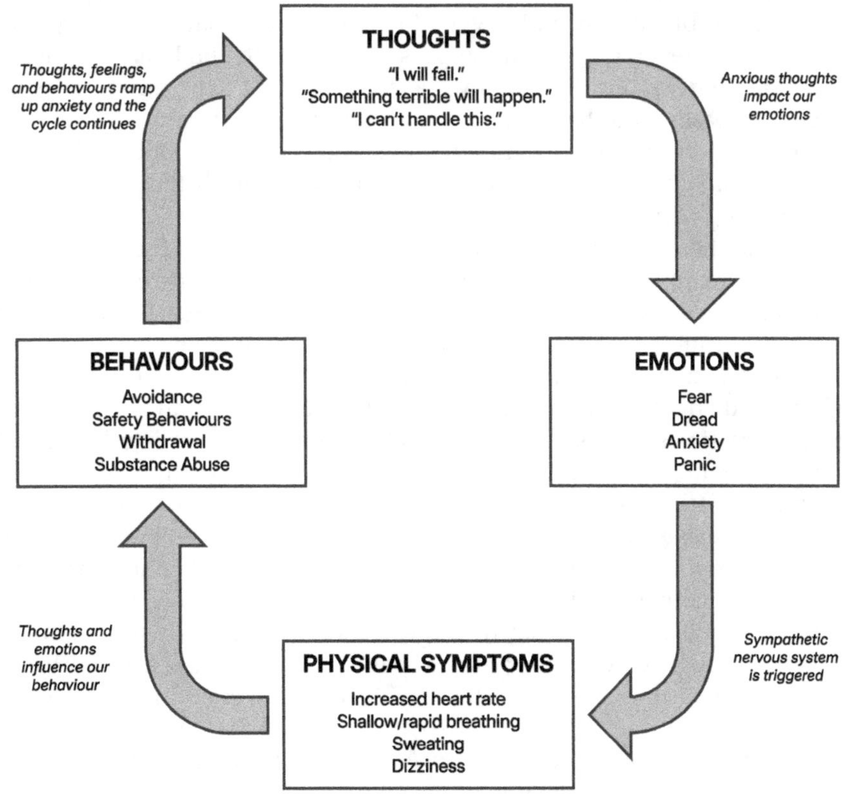

FIGURE 7.2

CBT thinking error cycle demonstrating how distorted thoughts, negative emotions and misinterpreted physical symptoms perpetuate maladaptive behaviours.

The behavioural component of CBT involves *desensitising* patients to the cues that trigger emotional distress. Exposure therapy is the gold standard for achieving this desensitisation (Foa and McLean, 2016). Exposure therapy requires patients to intentionally confront situations, objects or thoughts that trigger anxiety or fear while refraining from safety behaviours that decrease anxiety, fear or distress. Examples of safety behaviours include avoidance, using substances or medications to decrease anxiety or performing rituals.

Emotion processing theory explains how exposure therapy extinguishes fear and anxiety through desensitisation (Foa and Kozak, 1986). According to this theory, exposure to distressing or feared cues activates stored fear structures that trigger an intense fear response in the patient. As patients intentionally sit with this distress during exposure sessions, without performing safety behaviours, *habituation* occurs. Habituation refers to a decrease in anxiety that occurs naturally over time.

Excessive fear and anxiety result from overactivation of the sympathetic nervous system, which is responsible for the fight-or-flight response. Activation of this system increases heart rate, respiration and blood pressure. This increases blood flow and oxygen to muscles in preparation for fighting or fleeing. However, this activation puts a strain on the body and cannot be maintained indefinitely. Eventually, the activity of the sympathetic nervous system decreases, and the parasympathetic nervous system takes over. This system lowers heart rate, respiration and blood pressure, restoring the body to equilibrium and significantly decreasing anxiety. This is the physiological underpinning of habituation.

Exposure therapy produces habituation in real time. With the guidance of a seasoned therapist, patients are progressively exposed to increasingly more distressing cues and experience how distress naturally dissipates over time. Before performing exposures, the patient and therapist develop a list of cues and then rank them on a continuum of distress. The patient is started with the minimally distressing cues first, to allow them to build confidence in managing distressing situations. This approach avoids overwhelming the patient.

An important part of the exposure process is allowing distress to dissipate naturally. This allows the association between triggers and anxiety, fear or distress to weaken as patients experience habituation. It also breaks the link between fear and the behavioural response. Someone with a substance use disorder learns that cravings can dissipate without substance use. Patients with OCD realise that the strong urge to perform rituals will eventually weaken. Through repeated exposures, patients become desensitised to the trigger, meaning that over time, the cues provoke lower and lower levels of distress.

Habituation also promotes *inhibitory learning*, which is another component integral to the effectiveness of exposure therapy. Inhibitory learning occurs when the patient forms new beliefs regarding the feared situations or triggers (Craske et al., 2008). Exposure therapy allows patients to test their faulty thoughts or fear-based beliefs. By purposely encountering triggering cues and experiencing habituation, patients learn that the feared consequences do not occur. A patient with a public speaking phobia learns that the tremble in her voice and the flush of her cheeks do not result in people laughing at her and thinking that she is stupid. A patient suffering from contamination OCD realises that he is unlikely to catch a deadly virus from touching a doorknob with his bare hands.

Through exposure therapy, triggers that were once immensely distressing and fraught with fear become less and less triggering as patients form new associations with the triggers through repeated exposure. As patients complete exposure therapy, they are empowered by their mastery over the symptoms that have caused so much suffering. Through habituation and inhibitory learning, they begin to reframe anxiety and other negative emotional experiences as normal and temporary aspects of the human experience, rather than intolerable experiences to be avoided at all costs.

VR Factors Conducive to Exposure Therapy

The efficacy of exposure therapy can be enhanced by using VR to create immersive, multisensory, virtual exposure environments. In conventional exposure therapy, exposures are conducted by having patients imagine situations/triggers (imaginal exposure) or by creating exposures in real-world settings (*in vivo* exposures). VR introduces a level of immersion that makes the exposure response so much more effective than imaginal exposure. Verbally challenging distorted thoughts/beliefs produces a vastly different response physiologically and psychologically compared to confronting the situations a patient has spent a lifetime fearing. Exposures are systematically designed by therapists and patients to address the patients' triggers hierarchically, beginning with exposures that elicit mild or moderate distress and gradually working up to confronting the most feared triggers.

Though the efficacy of exposure therapy is well-established, patients may not benefit from it if they find the pace too overwhelming. Proceeding too quickly would be counterproductive, as the patient will withdraw and lose a sense of trust established with the therapist. Being able to finely tune the pace of exposure is very critical and is done more easily in VR than in the real world. Thus, VR is a powerful tool for patients who are hesitant or unwilling to engage in traditional exposure therapy. Studies have shown that many patients prefer virtual exposure therapy to more conventional techniques (Garcia-Palacios et al., 2007; Quero et al., 2014).

Additionally, VR can improve the cost-effectiveness of psychotherapy by reducing the number of sessions necessary to achieve meaningful improvements. Powers and Emmelkamp (2008) noted that patients moved more rapidly through their exposure hierarchies when they knew that they could leave the virtual exposure environment if necessary. These researchers also found that patients viewed virtual exposure therapy as having more potential to help them than traditional exposure therapy. Studies investigating the utility of VR exposure therapy for anxiety disorders have documented increased self-efficacy following virtual exposures (Cote and Bouchard, 2009; Meyerbroker et al., 2022; Powers and Emmelkamp, 2008). It is reasonable to suggest that these advantages could increase patients' engagement in treatment and empower faster recovery.

VR can be particularly useful for creating exposures that would be difficult, impossible or unethical to create in real-world settings. Conducting *in vivo* exposures with patients who have driving phobias comes with a host of logistical, liability and confidentiality issues. Similarly, how do you gather a crowd of people for public speaking exposure without the patient relinquishing confidentiality? Is it ethical to expose a patient with germ-related OCD to vomit or other bodily fluids that carry a real risk of contamination? VR not only makes these types of exposures possible but also allows therapists to manipulate parameters, like the number or gender of audience members or the degree of filth in a bathroom. In this way, fully immersive virtual environments can expose clients in real-time to their most distressing cues in a way that would be impossible or unethical using *in vivo* exposures.

Early adopters of VR technology in therapy questioned whether virtual environments could elicit the level of anxiety and distress required for successful exposure therapy. However, studies have shown that VR exposures evoke emotional responses as intensely or more intensely than traditional imaginal or *in vivo* exposures (Inozu et al., 2020; Laforest, Bouchard, Cretu and Mesly, 2016; Morina et al., 2015). In addition to eliciting fear and anxiety, virtual environments have been shown to trigger cravings for drugs and alcohol in people with substance use disorders, as well as impulses toward unhealthy eating behaviour in patients with eating disorders (Gorini et al., 2010; Perpiñá et al., 2001, 2013; Wiebe et al., 2022).

Another advantage of using VR for exposure therapy is that it often includes devices for measuring various physiological indicators of distress, like heart rate, heart rate variability, galvanic skin response and respiration rate. When not incorporated into a VR system, biofeedback devices can be cumbersome or distracting for patients, so they are not commonly used during *in vivo* exposure therapy. During traditional exposure therapy, therapists ask patients to rate their distress on a scale of 1–10. This Subjective Units of Distress scale, or SUD scale, enables therapists to monitor patients' emotional experiences as they proceed through the exposure. While therapists are skilled at using changes in a patient's facial expressions, body movements or affect to gauge emotional distress, the SUD scales offer a subjective (to the patient) rating of the patient's distress.

Measures of objective (physiological) and subjective distress are crucial for effective exposure therapy; these measures demonstrate habituation to patients. Exposure sessions continue until patients' distress dissipates,

TABLE 7.2

Summary of diagnostic category, fear and exposure concepts

Diagnostic Category	Fear or distress	Exposure Concept
Phobia	Phobic place, object or situation	Gradual introduction to the phobia in a controlled environment
Anxiety	Worry of situation	Target automatic thoughts rated to the worrisome situation
PTSD	Re-experiencing prior trauma	Confrontation with frightening, yet safe, stimuli
OCD	Loss of control related to obsession or compulsion	Re-experiencing of the trigger with coaching of response prevention
Substance use disorder	Recurrence of use	Triggers of "people, places and things"
Eating disorder	Relapse scenario	Feared food exposure, mirror exposure or family-based treatment with exposure

typically indicated by a reduction in SUDs score. The physiological measures offered with VR technology can be used alongside the SUDs scale to monitor emotional distress while providing objective, corroborating evidence for the patients. In cases where patients continue to report high levels of distress, decreases in physiological measures like heart rate, heart rate variability and respiration rate can be useful for showing physiological habituation.

The research described above has demonstrated the tremendous potential of VR for enhancing exposure therapy. VR can create immersive exposure environments for clients with fears or phobias that make *in vivo* exposure too difficult, costly, time-consuming or unsafe. When given the option, many patients prefer VR exposures. VR exposures are also more cost-effective than *in vivo* exposures that require extensive planning or traveling to exposure sites and patients may experience improvements with fewer exposure sessions.

Table 7.2 provides several examples of fears and exposure concepts for each diagnostic category. Exposure therapy operates on the principle of gradually confronting fears in a controlled environment, allowing patients to break the cycles of avoidance and distress. This framework underscores the broad applicability of exposure-based interventions in treating disorders driven by maladaptive fear responses.

Anxiety Disorders (e.g., Phobias, Agoraphobia, Social Anxiety Disorder)

The most well-established uses for VR in psychotherapy involve the treatment of anxiety disorders like specific phobias, agoraphobia and social anxiety disorder (Krijn et al., 2004; Wu et al., 2021). While every patient is unique and brings their specific fears and worries into therapy, patients struggling with anxiety disorders experience excessive fear and overestimation of risk/danger and engage in safety behaviours like avoidance. Research has shown that exposure therapy is effective in treating anxiety disorders (Mayo-Wilson et al., 2014; Ruhmland and Margraf, 2001; Wolitzky-Taylor et al., 2008).

Specific Phobia

Specific phobias are characterised by excessive fear or anxiety related to specific objects or situations (e.g., flying, heights, animals), including persistent avoidance of feared objects/situations. The fear and avoidance must be so severe that the patient cannot maintain social or personal relationships, work or engage in other meaningful activities (American Psychiatric Association, 2013). VR can enhance the effectiveness of exposure therapy for specific phobias by enabling patients to encounter feared objects/situations in an immersive virtual environment.

Imagine the difference between an imaginal exposure in which a patient with a snake phobia vividly imagines a snake encounter and a VR exposure in which a snake slithers towards a patient, rattle shaking. Flying phobias can prohibit people from taking jobs where travel is required or visiting friends and loved ones. Due to airport security and excessive costs, it is almost impossible to conduct *in vivo* exposures for flying but imagine being able to offer a patient a virtual experience of the entire flight process, from check-in, through security, boarding, take-off and landing, while having the capability to manipulate size of airport crowds, gender of security agents, noise levels and turbulence.

Several studies support the efficacy of VR exposure therapy for specific phobias (Cote and Bouchard, 2009; Meyerbroker and Emmelkamp, 2010; Meyerbroker et al., 2022). A meta-analysis of nine randomised clinical trials found that VR exposure therapy produced a large effect size for resolving phobias (Wechsler et al., 2019). Cote and Bouchard's study of VR exposure therapy for arachnophobia showed that after only five 60-minute sessions, patients reported increased self-efficacy and decreased anxiety. Importantly, these findings were corroborated by improved performance on a behavioural avoidance test, which shows that the gains made via immersive virtual environments generalise to real-world behaviour.

Social Anxiety Disorder

Social anxiety disorder is characterised by marked fear or anxiety related to social situations that involve potential scrutiny by others. Fears of negative evaluation cause people with social anxiety disorder to avoid social situations, performing in front of others or any situation in which they may be observed, which leads to substantial impairment in social and occupational functioning (American Psychiatric Association, 2013).

Creating exposures to treat this type of anxiety can be a logistical and ethical challenge, but VR can overcome these barriers. It is nearly impossible to protect patients' confidentiality while conducting effective *in vivo* public speaking exposures. Using VR, therapists can create exposures for patients to give presentations and speeches, engage in small talk at a party, interview for a job and so on. VR also allows the therapist to modify the exposure environment to create individually tailored exposures. With VR, it is possible to pause the interaction throughout, to allow the therapist to provide additional insights in real time. As the interaction progresses, various physical symptoms can lead to maladaptive or irrational thought patterns, and an astute therapist would use this as a teaching opportunity for the patient.

An important study comparing VR exposure therapy to group exposure therapy for social anxiety disorder showed that both treatments were effective (Anderson et al., 2005). Outcome measures for this study included self-ratings, a diagnostic interview and performance on a speech task. A follow-up study revealed that treatment gains were maintained at 4- to 6-year follow-ups, as indicated by speech task performance (Anderson et al., 2017). Moreover, a meta-analysis comparing VR exposure therapy to *in vivo* exposure therapy revealed that both treatments were effective, but twice as many people dropped out of *in vivo* exposure therapy (Wallach et al., 2009). These studies indicate that not only does VR exposure therapy lead to meaningful and durable decreases in social anxiety, but also its increased palatability to patients improves overall engagement.

Panic Disorder

VR can also be used to create effective and immersive exposures for patients with panic disorder. Panic disorder is often referred to as "fear of fear" and involves recurrent and unexpected panic attacks. Heart palpitations, sweating, trembling, dizziness, shortness of breath and fears of losing control, "going crazy" or dying are characteristic symptoms of panic attacks. People with panic disorder persistently worry about having panic attacks, and this worry leads to avoidance or other safety behaviours designed to prevent future attacks (American Psychiatric Association, 2013).

Interoceptive exposures are key to treating panic disorder. During interoceptive exposure, the bodily sensations that patients experience during panic attacks are intentionally induced. This allows patients to test their beliefs that the sensation is dangerous or harmful and enables them to habituate to the anxiety triggered by these sensations. Interoceptive exposures frequently involve spinning in a chair to elicit dizziness, breathing through a straw to trigger light-headedness, breathing rapidly to produce hyperventilation or exercising to elevate heart rate. Therapists coach patients to sit with the distress triggered by these sensations to demonstrate that the sensations and distress dissipate over time. Repeated exposure to the triggering bodily sensations allows patients to interpret them more realistically as normal physiological reactions rather than signs of impending death or disaster.

VR can be used to create the physiological sensations that trigger panic attacks in patients with panic disorder. Moreover, the immersive environment of virtual exposure may be more effective in provoking these triggers than the techniques used at home or in a therapist's office during more traditional exposure therapy. A meta-analysis revealed a large effect size for virtual exposure therapy for panic disorder when compared to a waitlist control or psychological placebo groups (Carl et al., 2019). Another study found that VR exposure therapy was as effective as *in vivo* exposure therapy and that the virtual exposures were rated as less aversive than *in vivo* exposures (Quero et al., 2014). This highlights VR's potential for improving therapeutic outcomes while lowering patients' fears about participating fully in the therapeutic process.

Agoraphobia

People with agoraphobia avoid situations like using public transportation, being in enclosed areas, standing in line or being in crowds, because they fear being unable to escape or get help if they panic (American Psychiatric Association, 2013). For people with severe agoraphobia, this fear becomes so great that they are unable to leave home. Agoraphobia can be challenging to treat because the journey between the home and the therapist's office is filled with triggers. Many patients with agoraphobia are reluctant to try exposure therapy because it feels too overwhelming. Virtual exposure therapy can provide access to an effective intervention for people who would otherwise decline treatment. A meta-analysis of exposure therapy for agoraphobia yielded similar effect sizes for *in vivo* and VR exposures (Wechsler et al., 2019).

PTSD

People who experience or witness actual or threatened death, serious injury or sexual or interpersonal violence are at risk for developing PTSD. PTSD is characterised by recurrent, intrusive and distressing memories of the trauma, negative emotional states, flashbacks, dissociation, hypervigilance, emotional numbing and avoidance of cues related to the traumatic event. PTSD is associated with significant suffering and impairment (American Psychiatric Association, 2013).

When trauma occurs, the brain shifts into survival mode, and impaired activity in the prefrontal cortex can hinder the ability to properly manage fear responses and suppress traumatic memories. As a result, these memories remain fragmented and easily accessible, leaving them vulnerable to evocation by a wide range of cues. Due to this, empirically supported treatments for PTSD require clients to recall traumatic events in as much detail as possible to identify cues that trigger PTSD symptoms. Prolonged exposure therapy and cognitive processing therapy, two empirically supported treatments for PTSD, require patients to generate detailed scripts of the trauma and to imagine re-experiencing the trauma as vividly as possible to facilitate appropriate emotional processing of the traumatic events (Sciarrino et al., 2020). When possible, the treatment also includes *in vivo* exposure to cues that elicit trauma memories or other PTSD symptoms.

Understandably, many people with PTSD are unwilling to engage in the daunting tasks involved in psychotherapy for PTSD. Emotional numbness is common in PTSD, wherein individuals feel disconnected from their emotions, detached from loved ones and lack interest in previously enjoyable activities. This protective response to overwhelming emotional pain can lead to isolation, difficulty forming relationships and a sense of being "cut off" from life. This also makes it difficult for patients to fully engage in the therapy. This withdrawal from life in the context of fragmented trauma memories adds another layer of difficulty in creating effective exposures.

VR may be particularly helpful for treating PTSD because the immersive nature of virtual environments can aid emotional engagement in a stepwise and progressive fashion. Virtual exposures are multi-sensory experiences that pull the patient into high engagement with traumatic experiences within the safety of a therapist's office or the patient's home. Traumatic events like combat or natural disasters present significant challenges for imaginal or *in vivo* exposure, but can be recreated in multi-sensory, immersive virtual environments.

Several studies have demonstrated that virtual exposures are effective for addressing trauma. Difede and colleagues (2007) used VR to treat 11 patients with PTSD resulting from the September 11, 2001 attacks. Ten patients completed treatment, which is impressive given that PTSD treatment often has high attrition, and nine of these patients experienced significant improvement. Given that five of these patients had previously completed intensive imaginal exposure therapy without improvement, this study shows that VR can be a powerful therapeutic tool for PTSD. Two studies investigating PTSD in combat veterans showed that virtual exposures were associated with significant improvements that were maintained at 3- and 6-month follow-ups (Ready et al., 2006; Rothbaum et al., 2001).

OCD

People with obsessive-compulsive disorder (OCD) experience highly distressing and impairing obsessions and compulsions. Obsessions are recurrent, persistent, unwanted and intrusive thoughts, urges or images that cause distress. Compulsions are repetitive behaviours or mental acts that people feel compelled to perform in response to an obsession. OCD involves a cycle in which obsessions cause significant distress, which the individual tries to lessen or neutralise with compulsions. Obsessions and compulsions are mutually reinforcing and, without treatment, significantly interfere with functioning. There are many different forms of OCD, but obsessions and compulsions often involve common themes like germs/contamination, checking/safety, symmetry, religion/scrupulosity and perfectionism (American Psychiatric Association, 2013).

Exposure and response prevention (ERP) is the empirically supported treatment for OCD (Öst et al., 2015). ERP requires patients to face their obsessions (the anxiety triggers) and refrain from performing rituals designed to counteract or neutralise the distress triggered by the obsessions. Breaking the connection between obsessions and compulsions allows patients to test their false beliefs about the meaning of the obsession and demonstrates that the feared outcomes do not occur.

For ERP to be successful, the exposures must provoke enough anxiety or distress that the patient can learn to tolerate distress without resorting to compulsions. However, in many instances, *in vivo* exposures are impossible, unethical or too risky. For example, the potential for harm or illness from exposures addressing contamination OCD is often prohibitive, as are the costs, travel time or safety risks involved in other types of *in vivo* exposures. In these instances, therapists must rely on imaginal exposure, which can reduce the efficacy of the treatment because many patients struggle to envision anxiety-provoking cues in a way that elicits the level of distress necessary.

ERP performed in VR can overcome many of the difficulties described above. Immersive, interactive, multisensory virtual environments make nearly any exposure possible. OCD is a highly individualised disorder, with each patient presenting with unique obsessions and compulsions. VR enables therapists to tailor exposure environments to meet the specific needs of patients. As patients progress through ERP, therapists can manipulate virtual environments to enhance treatment outcomes. Patients with the contamination type of OCD who begin ERP by entering and looking around dirty bathrooms can move on to touching faecal matter and other bodily fluids. Using VR exposures could go even further than would be possible with *in vivo* exposure, which could lead to enhanced outcomes.

Kim and colleagues (2008) demonstrated that virtual environments can provoke distress and checking behaviours in people with OCD. The exposure environment used in this study was a virtual apartment. These researchers compared the behaviour and anxiety levels of 33 people with OCD to 30 healthy, matched controls over three tasks. First, participants were instructed to navigate the virtual apartment as though they were getting ready for work. During this task, they were asked to flick on light switches, open windows and doors and turn on the gas burner on the stove and water faucets. Next, participants completed a distraction task. The third task was the focus of the experiment. Participants were told that they were free to check whatever they wanted within the apartment before leaving the exposure. The results of this study showed that people with OCD engaged in more checking than healthy controls. Additionally, anxiety scores before checking were significantly higher for participants with OCD. Furthermore, researchers found significant positive correlations between anxiety level after checking and the severity of OCD symptoms, general anxiety level and time spent checking for participants with OCD. This demonstrates that a virtual environment could elicit distress and prompt checking behaviour in people with OCD.

Research investigating the efficacy of VR exposure therapy for OCD is limited, but promising. Laforest, Bouchard, Cretu & Mesly (2016) showed that virtual environments are capable of triggering contamination obsessions and cleaning compulsions in people with contamination OCD. Another study from this research group investigated the impact of VR exposure therapy for three patients with contamination OCD. Exposures involved touching walls and toilet bowls with varying degrees of filth in a virtual environment, and the results indicated significant improvements in symptom severity after only eight sessions (Laforest, Bouchard, Bossé and Mesly, 2016).

Dua, Jagota and Grover (2021) present a case study that highlights how VR can be used to create highly specific, individualised virtual exposures to effectively treat OCD. The subject of this case study was a young man severely debilitated by intrusive and distressing images of familiar people. To neutralise the distress caused by the images, the young man performed repetitive actions like crossing thresholds at doors and handwashing rituals. The intrusive thoughts and rituals were severe and time-consuming; he lost his business and was unable to work despite previous efforts in imaginal exposure. VR was used to create a multi-sensory experience that included images and videos of the people featured in his intrusive thoughts, along with audio of his voice saying the people's names. Over repeated exposures, tolerating the distress provoked by this virtual environment without resorting to rituals led to clinically meaningful improvements in OCD symptoms. After treatment, the patient maintained an 80% improvement in OCD symptoms and was able to return to work.

The results of the studies described above indicate that VR can be a valuable addition to clinical practice for patients with OCD. VR seems particularly well-suited to ERP for OCD because it enables individually tailored exposures in which therapists can manipulate exposure parameters. Moreover, these studies suggest that using VR for ERP can increase patients' willingness to engage in exposures, decrease attrition and improve patient outcomes. Studies have shown that 50–60% of patients who complete traditional ERP for OCD show clinically significant improvement, which means that up to 40% of patients may only achieve minimal, if any, symptom improvement (Abramowitz et al., 2009; Eddy et al., 2004; Foa et al., 2005; Simpson et al., 2013). Additionally, in a review of studies on OCD, Abramowitz (2006) found treatment dropout rates ranging from 20% to 30%. Integrating VR into ERP could help address these issues.

The following case example describes Alex, a mother with severe contamination OCD, who uses virtual reality exposure therapy to gradually desensitise herself to kitchen and bathroom-related triggers, reducing compulsive cleaning and handwashing rituals that dominate her daily life.

Case Example: Alex

Alex is a 33-year-old mother of an 18-month-old who has struggled with contamination OCD for many years. Her symptoms recently increased significantly after her family contracted a stomach virus. Her obsessions and compulsions are so severe that she is having difficulty caring for her child. Her symptoms are most severe when she is in the kitchen or bathroom.

Preparing food for her family can take several hours, as she must wash every individual food item and sanitise her counters and sink several times throughout food preparation. Handling raw meat is especially difficult for her, as she experiences intrusive thoughts about salmonella and other food-borne illnesses. She has specific cutting boards for raw meat and a "raw meat knife," but once she has handled the meat, she feels compelled to wash her hands and sanitise her kitchen counters and sink. She also has obsessive thoughts about germs from the grocery store remaining on fruits and vegetables, so she washes them thoroughly with soap and then sterilises the counters and the sink and washes her hands again. Her obsessions about cleanliness were reinforced during the COVID-19 pandemic when news outlets emphasised the need for regular handwashing and other strategies to prevent illness.

She has an elaborate handwashing ritual whenever she handles food, uses the restroom or changes a diaper. First, she lathers soap by rubbing both hands together for 30 seconds. Then she gets a squirt of soap and washes each finger for 30 seconds, using a new squirt of soap for each finger. Once she has finished with her fingers, she washes her palms and the backs of her hands and then her wrists and forearms. This ritual takes about ten minutes, and she does this at least three times per meal she prepares. She uses Clorox wipes to wipe down her kitchen counters and the sink. The skin on her hands, wrists and forearms is dry and cracked and sometimes bleeds, due to her excessive washing. After a bowel movement, she feels compelled to clean the toilet with Clorox wipes. Every evening after bathing her child, she cleans the bathtub with Clorox wipes. She estimates that she spends over five hours per day washing and cleaning. She worries constantly that her child will get sick due to a lack of vigilance on her part.

Virtual reality exposure therapy would involve two exposure environments: a virtual kitchen and a virtual bathroom. Exposures would be hierarchically graded, beginning with less anxiety-provoking exposure tasks and progressing to the most highly distressing tasks. Virtual exposure environments would begin with touching and cutting fruits and vegetables on bare counters without engaging in handwashing or sanitising. Exposures would progress to handling and cutting meat, first on cutting boards and then on bare counters. The therapists could dial up the intensity of the exposures by including dirty-looking produce or pools of fluid under the raw meat. Exposure tasks would involve touching and handling "contaminated" foods, using the same knife and cutting board to cut raw meat and produce, and then preparing plates of food for the family. Alex would be instructed to abstain from washing, sterilising or any other behaviour that could decrease her anxiety, disgust or fear.

Exposure therapy for the obsessions and compulsions related to the bathroom could begin with a clean virtual bathroom. Alex would be asked to touch the toilet seat, the toilet water and then the sink and counters without washing or sterilising. The virtual environment could be modified to include increasing levels of filth, like urine or faeces on the toilet and dirty diapers on the floor. Alex would be asked to touch the toilet seat, the diapers on the floor and anything else that would trigger her obsessions, without engaging in washing or sanitising. A final virtual exposure could involve contaminating herself in a filthy virtual bathroom and then moving into the virtual kitchen to prepare food for her family without washing or sanitising. ERP can be challenging because there is often a healthy degree of obsession, in this case, washing hands. The ERP process is not supposed to prove that no handwashing is healthy, but allow the patient to become more comfortable in managing the distress when the strict regimen is not followed.

Immersion in these virtual environments will trigger intense fear and anxiety. Sitting with this distress and allowing it to naturally dissipate through habituation will weaken the association between the contamination obsessions and the compulsions. The virtual tasks described above will enable Alex to test her beliefs about the danger of "contaminated" food and surfaces in an individually tailored and safe environment. When psychotherapy is complete, the desensitisation and new learning gained from these exposures will generalise to Alex's lived experiences, and she will no longer spend hours washing and sanitising or agonising over intrusive thoughts. She will be empowered by her mastery over her anxiety and relieved to be able to care for her child without the interruptions caused by obsessions and compulsions.

Substance Use Disorders

Substance use disorders (SUDs) are characterised by persistent and escalating use of substances (e.g., alcohol, opiates, cannabis, cocaine), development of a tolerance to the substance, difficulty limiting intake and serious withdrawal symptoms when intake is discontinued or limited (American Psychiatric Association, 2013). People with SUDs experience negative affect and cravings when the substance they abuse is not available.

Cue exposure therapy, an important component of CBT for SUDs, involves exposure to substance-related cues while preventing patients from ingesting the substances. Using cues to elicit strong cravings and then preventing substance use helps extinguish the conditioned link between craving and consumption. Therapists coach patients through this process, encouraging them to use healthy coping skills to manage cravings and avoid relapse.

Cue exposure therapy can be enhanced by using VR to create exposure environments with increased *ecological validity*. Patients can interact in an immersive environment tailored to their pattern of substance use. The virtual environment can be modified to reflect specific locations (e.g., bars, parties, home), time of day (day versus night) and to include specific types of alcohol or drugs. The interactive nature of the virtual environment makes it possible for patients to handle peer pressure in realistic settings, rather than relying on role-playing with a therapist, which often does not translate well to triggering social situations in the real world.

Exposure to real-world cues and scenarios involving substance use is to be avoided at all costs, particularly early in treatment. In some cases, therapists may accompany patients to bars or restaurants for *in vivo* exposures, but these exercises are associated with a variety of confidentiality, ethical and liability issues. Additionally, there are safety concerns inherent to exposing patients to situations in which other people are engaging in substance use. Therefore, traditional cue exposure therapy for substance use disorders occurs in the therapist's office or possibly in a research laboratory. Despite efforts taken to make these settings resemble bars, parties or other places where people frequently use substances, these settings lack ecological validity.

Virtual environments, on the other hand, can be extremely realistic, heightening the reality of the exposure, which can lead to enhanced generalisation of desensitisation to real-world settings. Patients can be immersed in virtual bars, restaurants, dope houses or any other location associated with substance use, which would be likely to enhance the cravings elicited by these exposures. Evoking stronger cravings would enable patients to practise distress tolerance in realistic scenarios, increasing the likelihood that they will be able to resist substance use in real-world situations.

A systematic review found that VR cue exposure successfully elicits cravings across a range of substances, including alcohol, nicotine, cannabis and stimulants (Wiebe et al., 2022). Moreover, a meta-analysis of seven studies demonstrated that VR cue exposure therapy effectively reduced substance use and craving, improved treatment retention and has the potential to improve mood and anxiety disorder symptoms that commonly co-occur with substance use disorders (Taubin et al., 2022).

Hernandez-Serrano and colleagues (2020) examined the impact of adding VR cue exposures to treatment as usual for alcohol dependence. Patients in the VR cue exposure group completed six sessions of virtual exposures in which they were asked to observe and reach for alcoholic beverages while interacting in a variety of alcohol-rich environments. Patients who received this therapy were eighteen times more likely to experience improvements in alcohol cravings than those who received treatment as usual. Similarly, a study investigating the efficacy of VR conditioning on methamphetamine cravings found that patients who completed virtual exposures experienced significantly larger decreases in craving and heart-rate variability than waitlist controls (Wang et al., 2019).

VR can be a valuable clinical tool for eliciting cravings in a safe, but realistic, environment. VR exposures can be customised to simulate the locations in which patients previously used substances, complete with substance-specific triggers, like brands of alcohol or drug paraphernalia. These exposures provide patients with opportunities to build distress tolerance skills, weaken the link between triggers and cravings and improve self-efficacy regarding managing cravings without engaging in substance use.

The following case example describes Michael, a high-functioning financial analyst struggling with alcohol and cocaine addiction. Michael undergoes VR-based cue exposure therapy to confront his cravings in realistic virtual environments, strengthening his ability to resist substances in high-risk social settings.

Case Example: Michael

Michael is a 38-year-old financial analyst who works on Wall Street. He is in treatment for alcohol and cocaine addiction. Michael reports binge drinking (greater than five drinks in one sitting) at least four times per week and uses cocaine daily. Michael is professionally successful, but his wife left him last year due to his substance abuse. He worries that he will not be capable of maintaining his sobriety because an important part of his job involves taking potential clients out for drinks. He and his co-workers frequently stay out late in bars and clubs, using cocaine to stay awake and to combat fatigue during the workday.

VR-based cue exposure therapy could be helpful for Michael. Virtual exposure environments that realistically simulate the restaurants, bars and clubs could elicit strong cravings for alcohol and cocaine. Virtual exposures could be customised to involve specific cocktails that he frequently consumes. Similarly, VR enables realistic exposures to the bathrooms where he frequently uses cocaine. Bringing his therapist to his actual bathroom at work would be impossible without drawing concern and attention. VR accessories that provide olfactory input could be included to enhance his sense of presence in the triggering environment.

Triggering cravings in realistic virtual environments allows Michael to practise distress tolerance skills. As he learns to manage strong cravings without consuming substances, the association between triggers and cravings will weaken. He would be able to break the strong link between places (such as at work) and using cocaine. Additionally, Michael will feel more confident in his ability to maintain sobriety even if he experiences cravings. VR exposures allow for cue desensitisation in safe, ethical, ecologically valid and effective environments.

Eating Disorders

Eating disorders like anorexia nervosa, bulimia nervosa and binge-eating disorder involve a distorted body image, fears of being overweight, body dissatisfaction and unhealthy eating behaviour. These disorders cause tremendous suffering and are associated with high morbidity and mortality (American Psychiatric Association, 2013; Samnaliev et al., 2014; Treasure, 2012). While these disorders differ in terms of specific distortions and unhealthy behaviours, each involves intense emotional distress triggered by food-related cues. CBT is the treatment of choice for eating disorders, but as many as 50–60% of people do not fully respond to treatment (Södersten et al., 2017). Moreover, long-term recovery is difficult to maintain, as evidenced by the high relapse rates for these disorders.

Imaginal and *in vivo* exposure to food-related cues is one component of CBT for eating disorders. VR can enhance the ecological validity and effectiveness of cue exposure therapy for eating disorders. Virtual exposures may be superior for treating binge-eating disorder and bulimia because they can be tailored to include the specific foods patients binge and the locations where binges occur. Immersion in these environments enables patients to change how they respond to the distress provoked by food-related cues and helps prevent binge eating.

Additionally, drop-out rates tend to be high for eating disorder treatment. Body distortions and fears of gaining weight may be so severe that intentionally confronting triggering foods or situations feels too overwhelming. Virtual exposures may be an effective intermediary step between imaginal and *in vivo* exposure that could improve treatment retention by building self-efficacy via desensitisation to food-related virtual cues before facing these triggers in real-world settings.

Before investigating whether VR exposures can effectively desensitise people with eating disorders to food-related cues, it is necessary to demonstrate that virtual cues and virtual environments can trigger fear, anxiety and impulses to engage in unhealthy eating-related behaviour. The results of several studies have provided strong evidence that virtual environments elicit distress in people with eating disorders. Gorini and colleagues (2010) found that food presented within an immersive virtual environment elicited comparable emotional distress as real food for people with eating disorders and that distress triggered by real food and virtual food was greater than that elicited by photographs of food. A series of studies by Perpiñá and colleagues demonstrated that being asked to eat high-calorie foods like pizza and pastries while immersed in a virtual kitchen elicited anxiety, impulses to over-eat and moderate to extreme guilt in patients with bulimia and binge-eating disorder (Perpiñá et al., 2001). The addition of smell via augmented reality heightened these reactions (Perpiñá et al., 2013).

Ferrer-Garcia and colleagues (2017) examined the efficacy of VR cue exposure therapy in 64 patients with binge-eating disorder or bulimia who did not respond to structured CBT. Patients were randomised to receive additional CBT sessions or VR cue exposure therapy. These researchers found that VR cue exposure therapy was significantly more effective in reducing the frequency of binge and purge episodes, bulimia-related behaviours, drive for thinness and body dissatisfaction. A 6-month follow-up indicated that 70% of patients who received VR cue exposure therapy maintained abstinence from binge eating, compared to 26% of patients who received additional CBT sessions, suggesting that VR cue exposure therapy is a more effective second-line treatment (Ferrer-Garcia et al., 2019).

A small pilot study of adults who had previously received treatment for binge-eating disorder or bulimia demonstrated that all participants showed decreases in binge eating and purging after seven one-hour sessions of VR cue exposure therapy (Nameth et al., 2021). These researchers conclude that virtual environments may maximise inhibitory learning because patients can focus on urges to binge in a safely controlled environment where foods are not physically present. This weakens the association between the cue (food) and the conditioned response (bingeing).

The following case example describes Olivia, a lawyer battling anorexia, who engages in VR exposure therapy to face her fears of "dangerous" foods and body image concerns. Treatment with VR enables her to tolerate distress and challenge her restrictive eating behaviours.

Case Example: Olivia

Olivia is a 29-year-old lawyer who has been diagnosed with anorexia. She experiences intense body dissatisfaction, distorted body image, fears of gaining weight and is severely underweight due to restricting her food intake. Olivia reports intense anxiety when confronted with "dangerous" foods, like pizza, French fries and cake. She engages in extensive body checking after eating and purges whenever she feels "too full."

Virtual reality exposure therapy could help desensitise Olivia to food-related cues. Immersion in virtual environments containing "dangerous" foods would elicit intense distress and trigger safety behaviours like restricting, body checking or purging. Exposure to these cues without engaging in safety behaviours would weaken the link between these foods and unhealthy behaviour. Sitting with the distress and anxiety triggered by the cues until habituation occurs will demonstrate that even the most intense emotions eventually dissipate. These exposures also allow Olivia to challenge some of her food-related fears and beliefs and build self-efficacy regarding her ability to manage negative emotional states without engaging in unhealthy or self-destructive behaviour. Table 7.3 summarises the evidence base for VR exposure therapy across the disorders reviewed in this chapter.

TABLE 7.3

Summary of VR exposure therapy evidence by disorder

Disorder	Key Study	Design/N	Key Finding	Follow-up	VR vs. Trad.
Specific Phobia	Wechsler et al., 2019	Meta-analysis, 9 RCTs	Large effect size for phobia resolution	Varies	Comparable
Social Anxiety	Anderson et al., 2005; 2017	RCT; 4–6 yr follow-up	Equivalent to group exposure; gains were maintained	4–6 years	Comparable; lower dropout rate for VR
Panic Disorder	Carl et al., 2019; Quero et al., 2014	Meta-analysis; RCT	Large effect size vs. waitlist; less aversive than in vivo	Varies	Comparable; VR preferred by patients
Agoraphobia	Wechsler et al., 2019	Meta-analysis	Similar effect sizes for in vivo and VR	Varies	Comparable

TABLE 7.3 (Continued)

Summary of VR exposure therapy evidence by disorder

Disorder	Key Study	Design/N	Key Finding	Follow-up	VR vs. Trad.
PTSD	Difede et al., 2007; Ready et al., 2006	Open trial N=11; RCT	9/10 completers improved (incl. 5 non-responders to imaginal); gains were maintained	3–6 months	Effective for imaginal non-responders
OCD	Laforest et al., 2016; Dua et al., 2021	Case series N=3; case study	Significant symptom reduction in 8 sessions; 80% improvement maintained	Post-treatment	Promising; limited data
SUDs	Taubin et al., 2022; Hernandez-Serrano et al., 2020	Meta-analysis 7 studies; RCT	Reduced craving and use; 18x more likely to improve	Varies	Superior for cue elicitation
Eating Disorders	Ferrer-Garcia et al., 2017; 2019	RCT N=64	VR cue exposure superior to additional CBT; 70% vs. 26% abstinence at 6 months	6 months	Superior as a second-line treatment

Conclusion

Cue desensitisation via exposure therapy is an integral component of treatment for disorders that involve intense emotional distress to cues. Exposure therapy has a solid evidence base for reducing distress and avoidance while promoting adaptive behaviour, but many patients are hesitant or unwilling to engage in it. VR is particularly well-suited for exposure therapy because it allows for multisensory, highly realistic, immersive exposure experiences that are more cost-effective, easier to implement and preferred by many patients. Integrating VR into clinical practice for these disorders is likely to increase access to an effective intervention. Research has demonstrated that virtual exposure therapy is at least as effective as traditional exposure therapy across a broad range of mental health disorders, including anxiety disorders, PTSD, OCD, substance use disorders and eating disorders.

8

Cognitive Training

Introduction

Cognitive training interventions are integral to cognitive behavioural therapy (CBT) for many mental health conditions. A primary goal of these interventions is to help clients understand that thoughts and beliefs profoundly impact emotions and behaviours. Many individuals do not spend much time considering their thoughts or the beliefs underlying those thoughts; rather, they experience thoughts as automatic and outside of conscious control. Teaching patients to identify automatic thoughts is the first step towards gaining agency over those thoughts and reclaiming control over emotions and behaviours.

For many patients, cognitive training begins with building awareness of attentional resources. Our brains are hardwired to sift through an enormous onslaught of stimuli from the world around us and within us. Physical sensations are continuously being transmitted from sensory receptors in our skin through our nerves and carried to our brains. Our brains receive this mixture of stimuli, filter through it, sort relevant stimuli for further processing and ignore irrelevant stimuli. These processes are outside of our conscious awareness.

However, to notice something (a thought, a sensation, some aspect of the external environment), our attention must be directed to it. Humans have a limited attention span, which makes focused attention a valuable, but limited, resource. An important part of cognitive training involves teaching patients to be intentional about where they focus their attention. For people with chronic pain, this may involve a conscious shifting of attention away from pain onto something else. Patients with depression often focus only on the negative aspects of situations or experiences and need coaching to intentionally identify and focus on neutral or positive aspects. Similarly, people with anxiety disorders may focus solely on potentially threatening stimuli, while people with psychotic disorders may become fixated on irrelevant stimuli.

DOI: 10.1201/b23370-10

TABLE 8.1

Example CBT thought record used in cognitive restructuring: identifying negative automatic thoughts, generating alternative thoughts and re-rating mood

Situation (Who? What? Where? When?)	Mood (What do you feel?) Rate each 0–100%	Negative Automatic Thought (NAT) (What thoughts or images were going through your mind?)	Evidence supporting NAT	Evidence against NAT	Alternative thought (What is an alternative explanation or more balanced thought about this situation?)	Re-rate mood	Outcome
My friend texted me to cancel our plans for Friday night.	Anxious (60%) Depressed (50%)	"She doesn't want to be my friend." "She is angry with me."	She rarely cancels plans. She has seemed moody lately.	She said she hasn't been feeling well. She cancelled other weekend plans, too.	It's unlikely that she cancelled because she is mad or doesn't want to be my friend. It's more likely that she cancelled because she doesn't feel well.	Anxious (20%) Depressed (10%)	Return her call and ask if she needs anything and if we can reschedule. Call another friend and make plans for Friday night.

Another cognitive training strategy used by CBT therapists is *cognitive restructuring*. This intervention begins by teaching clients to identify (through focused attention) their *automatic thoughts*. These are the thoughts that come to mind quickly and without effort. Automatic thoughts are often triggered by deeply held, but distorted, beliefs that people hold regarding themselves, other people or the world. Once these thoughts and beliefs are identified, therapists and patients work together to understand how they impact emotions and behaviours. Patients are asked to track automatic thoughts by observing and recording thoughts triggered in specific situations and how those thoughts impact mood, emotions and behaviours.

Through cognitive restructuring, such as in Table 8.1, therapists highlight unhealthy patterns of thinking and unhelpful or untrue beliefs, and patients observe the destruction wrought by these patterns. Therapists teach patients how to challenge these thoughts and beliefs by finding confirming or disconfirming evidence. These exercises help patients develop more cognitive flexibility by identifying alternative explanations. Patients are encouraged to replace their automatic thoughts and beliefs with those that are more accurate and adaptive. As patients complete these exercises, both in therapy and in their everyday lives, they are empowered by how the techniques they have put in place improve their mood and lead to healthier, more adaptive behaviour.

Pain Management

The gate-control theory of pain (Melzack and Wall, 1965) redefined conceptualisations of pain. Before this theory, pain was assumed to result from a linear process whereby painful stimuli received by the peripheral nervous system were translated into neural impulses that travelled directly to the brain. However, this conceptualisation did not capture the complex nature of pain and could not explain the psychological aspects of pain. The gate-control theory challenged this simplistic conceptualisation by positing "gatelike" neural mechanisms located in the spinal cord that could "open" to allow transmission of pain signals to the brain, or "close" to prevent signal transmission. The most important contribution of this theory was the realisation that the state of these gates (open vs. closed) was modulated by many factors, including emotions, psychological states and previous experiences. The gate-control theory captured the nuances of pain and explained how pain could be exacerbated by previous trauma or current psychological distress.

In the decades since the gate-control theory was proposed, our understanding of how the brain processes pain has increased considerably. We now know that neural mechanisms involved in nociception (pain perception) are much more complex than originally proposed. However, the central tenets of the gate-control theory have stood the test of time. Put simply, gating mechanisms in the spinal cord can facilitate or inhibit the flow of pain signals to the brain, and cognitive and affective processes impact pain perception (Thorn, 2021).

The gate-control theory of pain spurred interventions designed to "close" the gate, thereby inhibiting the transmission of pain signals to the brain. Some interventions used ice or heat to provide contradictory sensory information to close the gate, while more effective interventions focused on harnessing thoughts and behaviours to modulate pain. These interventions involve distraction techniques designed to shift attention away from pain and cognitive restructuring to harness the power of thoughts in changing emotions and behaviour.

Distraction Techniques

Distraction works because attention is a finite resource. Experiencing pain requires attention to pain; focusing a larger portion on something other than pain means that a smaller portion is available to attend to pain, which decreases the experience of pain. In the parlance of the gate-control theory, shifting attention away from pain closes the gate, reduces the transmission of pain signals to the brain and diminishes the experience of pain. VR is particularly effective for distraction because it is immersive. Not only does it give patients something else to focus on, but it also blocks visual and auditory stimuli from the environment, thereby limiting the amount of incoming negative, pain-related stimuli and reducing pain-related cues.

VR has tremendous potential for acute pain management. A systematic review of studies investigating VR as an adjunctive treatment to manage pain in burn patients highlights the potential of this technology (Luo et al., 2018). Burn patients experience some of the most excruciating levels of pain, and this pain is repeatedly exacerbated in the acute course of treatment. Not only do the burns themselves result in pain, but frequent dressing changes and repeated daily physical therapy also inflict continued extreme levels of pain. Analgesic pain medications have many side effects, including the risk of respiratory depression and oversedation, and are often ineffective in completely relieving the pain suffered by burn victims. Luo and colleagues showed that adding VR to analgesic medications led to greater reductions in pain intensity, unpleasantness and time spent thinking about pain during dressing changes or physical therapy sessions than analgesic medications alone (Luo et al., 2018).

Oncology is another area where the inclusion of VR could improve patients' experiences and outcomes. Although cancer pain is often thought of as a chronic pain condition, survivors will tell you there are many experiences of acute pain from surgery, port placement or access, or other procedures such as lumbar punctures. As many as 50% of cancer patients who experience pain do not receive adequate pain relief, which can complicate treatment and lead to deteriorating health (Wiederhold et al., 2014). VR could help manage pain at each of these levels.

Cancer treatment providers have long recognised the value of distraction as an effective pain management technique. Patients are often encouraged to read, watch movies, listen to music or play games during hospitalisations or while receiving treatments to take their minds off their current situation. An immersive technology like VR could be infinitely more effective for distraction. Consider the difference between listening to music, watching a movie on your phone or reading a book, and being immersed in a multisensory virtual environment. VR not only engages the senses, but it also blocks out the immediate physical surroundings. The sight of medical professionals, other patients or infusion lines and needles can be replaced with a visually appealing virtual world. Beeping machines, hushed conversations and hospital noise give way to the peaceful sounds of the ocean. Instead of forcing yourself to focus on the words on a page or struggling to engage your mind in a board game, you could now be inside that game, or sitting on the beach, watching the tide roll in and listening to the soothing rush of water.

The first study investigating VR for oncology found significant decreases in negative emotions, pain and anxiety reported by a patient who used VR during chemotherapy infusion (Oyama et al., 1999). This finding ignited research into how VR can enhance cancer treatment outcomes. In a review of 19 studies, Chirico and colleagues (2016) highlighted that all the reviewed studies found reductions in stress and perceived distress when cancer treatment incorporated VR. Physiological data collected by sensors embedded in the VR technology corroborated these reductions, including decreases in heart rate. An additional systematic review bolstered the evidence supporting the efficacy of VR for enhancing cancer care. This review found strong evidence of decreased pain and anxiety in children and adolescents undergoing painful cancer-related procedures and adults who were hospitalised with cancer or receiving anticancer treatments when VR was added to standard care (Ahmad et al., 2020). These researchers concluded that VR technology should be considered an adjunctive intervention for managing pain and anxiety during cancer treatment.

It is important to note that VR confers benefits with very little or no risk to patients; patients are not required to undergo training or additional painful procedures, and VR does not add significant expense to the treatments. It is reasonable to assume that the decreases in distress, pain and anxiety, along with increases in well-being reported by patients using VR, could translate into improved treatment outcomes and increased life expectancy. Research has demonstrated that reductions in depression are associated with longer survival in patients with metastatic breast cancer (Giese-Davis et al., 2011). Reductions in pain, anxiety and distress could also be related to increased long-term survival for cancer patients. Interventions like VR that improve patients' experience ought to be the standard of care in oncology.

These studies supporting the acceptability, feasibility and efficacy of using VR for pain management in cancer patients suggest that VR could be more widely implemented to address a variety of patient concerns. Many conditions require patients to receive infusions or undergo painful or anxiety-provoking tests or procedures. Imagine the utility of VR for distracting children who need several vaccinations yet are fearful of needles or for lowering anxiety and distress in patients before an MRI or other imaging procedure.

Several studies have investigated the feasibility and utility of implementing VR more broadly in healthcare settings. One study compared reductions in pain for inpatients with a variety of conditions who reported average pain scores of at least 3 on a scale of 1–10. Compared to a control cohort who watched a 2D video, patients who used immersive 3D VR reported greater pain reduction; 65% of the VR cohort experienced clinically significant reductions in pain with no adverse effects from using VR (Tashjian et al., 2017).

Chronic Pain

CBT is an evidence-based treatment for chronic pain (Butler and Moseley, 2013; Ehde et al., 2014; Hoffman et al., 2007; Williams et al., 2012). In this form of CBT, therapists begin by explaining how thoughts and beliefs about pain can impact the experience of pain. The gate-control theory is presented to explain strategies that can help manage pain. Therapists help patients identify negative automatic thoughts and core beliefs that lead to negative emotional experiences and behaviours that can maintain or intensify pain. For example, daily physical exercise has been shown to improve many types of chronic pain, like fibromyalgia and rheumatoid arthritis. However, many patients do not engage in physical activity due to fears that exercise will worsen their pain. CBT therapists help patients understand how this belief reinforces incapability, helplessness and avoidance behaviour. Many chronic pain patients become depressed from the stress of experiencing daily pain. This leads to withdrawal and social isolation, which intensifies both negative emotions and pain. CBT therapists also help patients identify distorted thoughts and beliefs (e.g., pain = harm) that maintain this cycle, challenge these thoughts/beliefs and replace them with more adaptive thoughts/beliefs. Changes in thoughts and beliefs increase engagement in meaningful and enjoyable activities, which improves mood and reduces pain.

Most research investigating the utility of VR interventions for pain has focused on distraction during acute pain, but companies like AppliedVR (https://www.appliedvr.io) have developed VR programs for managing chronic pain. Early research on these applications is promising. A randomised clinical trial investigated the feasibility of a self-administered VR program that incorporated CBT-based skills for chronic pain (Darnall et al., 2020). Participants in this RCT were adults with chronic low back pain or fibromyalgia who reported an average pain score of over 4 for at least the past month, with pain that had persisted for at least six months. The 21-day skills-based immersive VR program was associated with a significant reduction in pain. Participants were highly engaged in the program and reported satisfaction upon completion, suggesting that these types of VR programs have great potential to enhance current interventions for chronic pain.

While research is limited, VR interventions could be designed to help patients combat the negative thoughts and beliefs surrounding their pain. VR games can be used to boost mood, engage patients in safe exercise and build self-efficacy. As patients continue to participate, they would be likely to experience improvements in mood and pain, which would provide powerful contradictory evidence for many of the thoughts and beliefs they have developed regarding chronic pain. When combined with mindfulness, relaxation training and other interventions, VR interventions could enhance current treatments for chronic pain without adding additional medications or risks.

VR could be used to reduce pain and distress in people suffering from a wide variety of chronic or acute conditions. Research has consistently shown that VR is an effective distraction from pain, often resulting in decreased pain, anxiety and depression and improved well-being. These findings are significant and could greatly improve outcomes and life expectancy for chronic conditions. Additionally, compared to pain medications, VR is associated with few side effects or risks to the patient and can be implemented without significantly increasing the cost of care.

Eating Disorders

The cue-desensitisation section noted that eating disorders like anorexia nervosa and bulimia nervosa are associated with high mortality from increased health problems, suicide and high rates of relapse. Researchers and clinicians have noted that while treatments like CBT are effective in changing eating-related thoughts and reducing unhealthy behaviours, body image distortions and body dissatisfaction often persist. These distortions are central to the maintenance of eating disorders and predict relapse and other poor outcomes (Carter et al., 2004; Farrell and Shafran, 2006; Stice, 2002).

The Allocentric Lock Theory explains the persistence of body image distortions and body dissatisfaction despite changes in one's thoughts and behaviours (Dakanalis et al., 2016; Riva, 2014). According to this theory, the unhealthy attempts at weight control (fasting, vomiting, abusing laxatives) that are common to anorexia, bulimia and binge eating disorder are triggered by negative body-related memories and experiences that have been reinforced and strengthened by social and cultural factors. These memories and beliefs are resistant to change, despite other treatment gains, because individuals with eating disorders have perceptual processing impairments that prevent them from being updated.

This means that no matter what they do, no matter how much weight they lose, despite ceasing the binge/purge cycle and establishing healthy eating patterns, their brains do not update their body representations to reflect the current reality. They are "locked into" a false idea of themselves that pushes them to take even more dangerous and extreme steps to manage the distress caused by allocentric, outdated body representations. For people with anorexia, this may be increasingly extreme dietary restraint, while for people with bulimia or binge eating disorder, this could lead to the complete revocation of restraint and escalating bingeing/purging cycles.

VR could be the key to unlocking this aspect of eating disorders. Using VR to construct embodied virtual avatars for patients with eating disorders is a central component of Experiential Cognitive Therapy (ExCT) developed by Giuseppe Riva's research group in Milan (Riva et al., 1998). ExCT combines a cognitive-behavioural approach with a VR protocol to address body image disturbances, motivation, self-efficacy, self-acceptance and control of eating behaviour. Multiple studies conducted by this research group have found that ExCT is effective in improving body image, satisfaction and self-efficacy (Riva et al., 2001, 2002, 2003, 2006).

The VR protocol included in ExCT asks patients to identify situations associated with the development of negative body image (e.g., getting teased by peers in the lunchroom). Using open-source software (NeuroVR), these situations are re-created virtually. VR therapy begins with patients virtually re-experiencing these events from a first-person perspective; patients cannot see their bodies. During these sessions, therapists coach patients to use cognitive restructuring to correct negative body-related thoughts and beliefs and replace emotional labels ("worthless") with more descriptive and accurate words. As sessions progress, patients virtually re-experience the events from a third-person perspective, which allows them to see their bodies in the scene. Patients calm and reassure their virtual avatars and counter the negative evaluations of others within the scenario. Therapists use Socratic questioning to help patients identify and correct aspects of the painful experience. For example, the therapist may ask the patient how the situation would look to an observer or ask the patient to act as the observer to directly address the painful elements of the scenario by correcting the negative evaluations of the avatar. The patient is asked to consider what would be necessary, within that moment, to help their avatar feel better and to offer that consolation.

Riva and colleagues (2002) examined the efficacy of ExCT for patients diagnosed with binge eating disorder. The results of this study demonstrated the superiority of ExCT for improving overall psychological health, including increasing body satisfaction, self-efficacy and motivation for change. Additionally, an RCT comparing ExCT to CBT and a nutrition group demonstrated the superiority of ExCT for binge-eating disorder; 77% of patients who completed ExCT quit bingeing, compared to 56% for CBT and 22% for the nutrition group. Moreover, ExCT was associated with improved scores on a body image assessment and an eating disorder inventory (Riva et al., 2003). These results show that, unlike CBT, ExCT addressed and corrected body image distortions.

Cesa and colleagues (2013) also tested the effectiveness of ExCT compared to CBT and an inpatient multimodal treatment program for morbidly obese patients with binge-eating disorder. In this study, CBT involved self-monitoring exercises to identify high-risk situations that trigger binge eating, education and support in healthy eating patterns, training in managing high-risk situations and relapse prevention. ExCT consisted of traditional CBT plus 15 sessions using Riva's VR protocol over five weeks. The results of this study support the Allocentric Lock Theory by showing that even though both traditional CBT and ExCT were effective for maintaining low monthly rates of binge eating episodes, only ExCT was effective at improving weight loss at a one-year follow-up. These findings indicate that the VR protocol helped patients "unlock" their faulty, negative body-related memories, which allowed them to update their body representations and maintain treatment gains.

Further support for the Allocentric Lock Theory is provided by studies that use VR to create a full-body illusion (FBI). Keizer and colleagues (2016) speculate that the persistence of body image distortions despite treatment with CBT may reflect the multisensory experience of distortions in body size. Perhaps the inability to update body representations posited by Allocentric Lock Theory is due to the failure of CBT interventions to capture the lived experience of these inaccurate body representations, size distortions and body dissatisfaction. FBI enables patients to embody a complete, fake virtual body; this body is perceived and regarded as their own physical body (Keizer et al., 2016; Porras-Garcia et al., 2021; Riva et al., 2003). Therapists can adjust the height, weight, circumference and other aspects of the embodied virtual bodies to target fears of gaining weight, image distortions and body dissatisfaction to promote self-acceptance.

Keizer and colleagues (2016) used VR to compare the impact of FBI on female patients with anorexia to healthy females. In this study, participants provided size estimates of various body parts (shoulders, abdomen, hips and height) before and after engaging in an FBI where they embodied a virtual female body with a healthy body mass index (BMI). As expected, before the FBI, participants with anorexia consistently overestimated their body size to be wider and rounder. Following the FBI, the percentage of misestimation produced by participants with anorexia decreased, but had not normalised to the estimates given by healthy females.

A similar study compared CBT for eating disorders with and without a VR component to address body image distortions and found greater improvement for patients who completed the virtual component (Marco et al., 2013). Improvements were maintained at a one-year follow-up, which is significant given the role of body image disturbances in relapse. Furthermore, completion of the virtual component was also associated with improvements in depression, anxiety and negative emotions.

Porras-Garcia and colleagues (2021) used the FBI to address fears of gaining weight and body image distortions in patients with anorexia. In this study, participants began by embodying virtual bodies that matched their actual size. Small increases in BMI were applied to these virtual bodies as VR sessions progressed until reaching a healthy BMI. Compared to a control group, participants who completed the virtual sessions reported significantly lower levels of body dissatisfaction, body distortions and fears of gaining weight. Virtual sessions were also associated with increased body appreciation and a decrease in other eating disorder symptoms. A 3-month follow-up showed maintenance of treatment gains.

The results of these studies provide strong support for using VR to enhance treatment for eating disorders. Given the high relapse rate and significant mortality risk associated with these disorders, the clinically significant improvements observed in these studies are particularly impressive. Eating disorder specialists and people with eating disorders have long noted that distorted body image and body dissatisfaction are extremely resistant to change, even with the normalisation of eating behaviour. The multisensory embodied VR-based interventions may be the key to helping patients overcome these difficulties, perceive their bodies more accurately and improve body image.

Case Example: Olivia (continued)

Despite improvements in her eating behaviour and weight following VR-based exposure therapy, Olivia continues to report high levels of body dissatisfaction, distorted body image and fears of gaining weight. Experiential cognitive therapy can effectively target these remaining symptoms. As part of this intervention, Olivia recalls that the first time she felt ashamed of her body was when her stepdad called her "chunky" at the family dinner table and suggested that she eat smaller portions. Olivia's therapist re-creates this scene in a virtual environment and coaches Olivia through confronting this painful memory.

Over the course of several virtual sessions, Olivia re-experiences this event from a first-person perspective. With support from her therapist, she uses cognitive restructuring to correct her negative thoughts and beliefs about her body and replaces the labels she has incorrectly applied to herself ("too much" and "unlovable") with healthier and more accurate terms ("worthy" and "enough"). In later virtual sessions, she re-experiences this event from a third-person perspective that allows her to watch herself in the scene while offering comfort and validation to her avatar.

Olivia's therapist further targets her distorted body image and fears of gaining weight via the full-body illusion. During these sessions, Olivia embodies a virtual body while her therapist adjusts the weight, size and circumference of various body parts until a healthy BMI is reached. This embodied experience resets Olivia's body representation, allowing her to update her representation of herself and see herself more accurately. Upon completion of experiential cognitive therapy, not only has Olivia's eating behaviour and weight stabilised, but her body image is also more accurate, she reports higher body satisfaction and her fears of gaining weight have subsided.

Psychotic Disorders

Schizophrenia spectrum and other psychotic disorders are among some of the most distressing and debilitating mental health conditions. These disorders are characterised by abnormalities in at least one of the following areas: delusions, hallucinations, disorganised thinking, disorganised or abnormal motor behaviour and negative symptoms. The *positive symptoms* of schizophrenia, like delusions and hallucinations, are considered excesses; they reflect experiences that go beyond what is considered typical in a given culture. *Negative symptoms*, on the other hand, reflect the absence of typical behaviour and include diminished emotional expression, significant reductions in purposeful activities (avolition), loss or substantially diminished experiences of pleasure (anhedonia) and reduced speaking (alogia). While the positive symptoms are more prominent and visibly distressing, especially to other people, the negative symptoms significantly contribute to the severe deficits in functioning often associated with these disorders (American Psychiatric Association, 2013).

Since the 1950s, antipsychotic medications have been used to treat psychotic disorders. These medications are effective in diminishing delusions and hallucinations to varying degrees but cause significant side effects and often have little or no impact on negative symptoms. Between 25% and 50% of patients treated with antipsychotic medications continue to experience persistent psychotic symptoms (Gould et al., 2001). Treatment for psychotic disorders often involves a team of mental health professionals, including psychiatrists for medication management, therapists who provide psychotherapeutic interventions and social workers or community mental health workers who focus on social skills, job training and addressing problems of daily living.

Once research established CBT as the treatment of choice for depression, anxiety disorders and other mental health conditions, clinicians began tailoring CBT to meet the specific needs presented by psychotic disorders. CBT for psychosis, or CBTp, operates from the same cognitive-behavioural framework as treatments for depression and anxiety disorders. CBTp emphasises the importance of developing a strong therapeutic relationship between the therapist and the client. This is critical for patients who have experienced considerable stigma related to psychotic experiences and whose symptoms make them particularly vulnerable to feeling misunderstood, targeted or invalidated.

The goals of CBTp change over time as the patient develops more insight into the condition. In the initial, first break of psychosis, the goal might be to achieve stabilisation of distress, minimising self-harm, violence toward others and attending to basic needs such as eating and sleeping regularly. In the active phase of illness, symptoms are severe, and the patient might have no understanding of what delusions or hallucinations are. Much psychoeducation would need to be done to help improve a patient's understanding of psychosis. The therapist should focus on the patient's safety and building an alliance before introducing VR to a patient with psychosis who has no insight.

Once a strong alliance has been established, CBTp therapists work with clients to normalise the symptoms that patients experience. Rather than labelling auditory hallucinations or persecutory delusions as atypical or outside the realm of normal experience, therapists educate clients about the number of people who experience these phenomena from time to time. Therapists also draw connections between situations that can exacerbate these symptoms, like stress, sleep deprivation, substance use or trauma, to set the stage for identifying alternative beliefs about these experiences.

Therapists help clients understand that it is not the actual symptoms themselves that cause impairments in functioning or damage to well-being, but the distress generated by the symptoms. Many people experience occasional voices or uncharitable thoughts about the motives of others, but these experiences do not elicit intense emotional distress, in part because of the beliefs attached to these experiences. For several reasons, hallucinations and delusions trigger intense emotional distress in people with psychotic disorders who have previously been told or have been made to feel as though these experiences prove that they are abnormal or "crazy." One of the primary goals of CBTp is reframing the beliefs patients hold about their symptoms to reduce the distress elicited by them. Normalising these experiences and helping patients identify alternative explanations for them are powerful tools that lead to decreased distress and increased functioning and quality of life.

In the early stages of CBTp, therapists may teach clients distraction techniques to cope with hallucinations or delusions. Therapists help patients learn to shift their attention away from the voices or troubling thoughts by encouraging them to listen to music, engage in creative pursuits like painting, talk to a friend or use guided imagery to create a safe space (Sivec and Montesano, 2012). As discussed in previous sections, immersive VR environments can be used for distraction, particularly early in therapy when voices or thoughts are intense and difficult to ignore. Multisensory virtual environments can provide a respite from these symptoms while allowing patients to practise meditation or relaxation exercises.

Persecutory Delusions

As many as 70% of patients with schizophrenia or psychotic disorders experience persecutory delusions (Freeman and Garety, 2014). Beliefs that other people are trying to harm them contribute to the desire to withdraw from social interactions and isolate, which interferes with their ability to work or maintain relationships. They may also act in erratic and irrational ways based upon these fears, leading to potential legal consequences. Avoidance and isolation remove the possibility of testing these paranoid beliefs and limit opportunities to experience positive emotions, which exacerbates symptoms and further decreases the quality of life. CBTp has demonstrated efficacy in reducing persecutory delusions, but a recent meta-analysis yielded only a small-to-medium effect size and indicated that nearly half of patients do not benefit from this treatment (Van der Gaag et al., 2014).

There are also practical barriers that impede the utility of CBTp for many patients. The behavioural exercises designed to test patients' persecutory beliefs are often overwhelming and distressing for patients, leading them to avoid the very treatment shown to be most effective. Additionally, designing these exercises is time-consuming for therapists, which can lead to improper implementation. Conducting behavioural exercises in the real world, where people often behave in unpredictable or unhelpful ways, can be risky. Imagine convincing a client to test his belief that everyone is out to harm him by taking him to a store and then standing by helplessly as that patient is taunted or insulted by a customer or sales associate. Rather than challenging their paranoia, the experience would likely cement this belief and cause further withdrawal.

VR can be used to address the limitations of traditional CBTp, leading to enhanced treatment outcomes. Using VR, patients can repeatedly practise difficult activities specifically designed to trigger their anxiety and persecutory beliefs. Patients can practise navigating these environments with feedback and coaching from therapists in real-time. Patients who are reluctant to engage in real-world exercises are more likely to engage in virtual encounters, knowing that they can remove the VR headset at any time. Additionally, therapists can adjust the characteristics of the social environment by manipulating the gender, number and ethnicity of the avatars populating the virtual environment. As patients gain confidence and skills, therapists can increase the difficulty of the exposures by increasing the suspiciousness or level of threat displayed by avatars.

Freeman and colleagues (2016) conducted a randomised controlled experimental study to investigate how VR could enhance psychotherapy targeting delusional conviction. Thirty participants with persecutory delusions were randomised to receive either virtual reality cognitive therapy or virtual reality exposure therapy. The intent of the VR cognitive therapy was to have participants test threat beliefs in VR environments without engaging in safety behaviours. In the VR exposure condition, participants confronted situations that provoked threat beliefs but were allowed to keep safety behaviours. Compared to the VR exposure condition, VR cognitive therapy was associated with large decreases in delusional conviction and real-world distress. These results indicate that VR environments can produce changes in beliefs and new learning that generalises to improved functioning in real-world settings.

Berkhof and colleagues (2021) reported on a preliminary randomised controlled trial comparing virtual reality-based CBTp to treatment as usual for persecutory delusions. They found that, while adding a VR component increased the initial cost of the treatment, the VR-based CBTp group had lower health care costs and accrued fewer costs due to loss in productivity at a 3-month follow-up. Importantly, the VR-CBT group had zero psychiatric admission days at follow-up. This research group is currently conducting a larger study comparing VR-based CBTp to standard CBTp.

Auditory Hallucinations

Auditory verbal hallucinations (AVH) are the most common form of hallucinations experienced by people with psychotic disorders (Landmark et al., 1990). As with other positive symptoms of psychotic disorders, antipsychotic medications fail to help many patients with AVH, and individuals may be prone to side effects. AVH that are derogatory in nature could increase the risk for self-harm. Additionally, only about half of patients respond favourably to CBTp, the treatment recommended for AVH. This means that many patients, despite serious efforts to address their symptoms, continue to experience persistent and disabling AVH.

VR can be used to create experiential and exposure-based interventions that surpass those designed as part of traditional CBTp. One of the primary goals of CBTp for AVH is to change the relationship between patients and the voices they hear. As previously noted, it is not the experience of the voice that causes impairment, but the patient's beliefs about the voice and the emotions triggered by the experience. Patients often describe AVH as scary, condemning and highly distressing. Over time, many patients come to accept what the voices are saying as truth. CBTp involves therapists and patients collaborating to change how patients relate to their voices, regulate negative emotions elicited by the voices and strengthen patients' sense of self.

One of the challenges of CBTp is that the voices are not real, so exposure to the voices is impossible. However, VR can be used to generate voices that mimic patients' symptoms, allowing the patient to engage with the voices in real-time in a safe and controlled environment. AVATAR therapy (AT) and VR-assisted therapy (VRT) are two ways that VR has been incorporated into CBTp for AVH. In these types of VR therapy, patients create and personalise the face and voice of an avatar that mimics the entity or person they believe to be the source of their distressing voices. While immersed in the VR environment, patients engage in dialogue with these avatars as the avatars confront them with personalised voices. This allows patients to practise using coping skills to manage distress triggered by the voices and to correct or argue against what the voices are saying. As therapy progresses, the avatars become less hostile, which builds empowerment in patients. Repeated practice enables patients to become assertive with their voices and increases self-esteem. VR sessions may be recorded, and therapists can encourage patients to listen to the sessions on their own, particularly when they experience voices.

A 7-week clinical trial comparing VR therapy to therapy as usual for AVH showed that VR therapy produced significant reductions in the severity of AVH and depressive symptoms and increased quality of life (Du Sert et al., 2018). These gains were maintained at a 3-month follow-up. Researchers concluded that the therapeutic effect of VRT was achieved via the reduction of distress associated with AVH. A larger RCT comparing AT to supportive counselling for persistent AVH found that 12 weeks of AT resulted in significant reductions in AVH severity (Craig et al., 2018). AT included six weekly 50-minute sessions in which patients engaged in 10–15 minutes of face-to-face virtual interactions with their avatars. Therapists encouraged patients to speak directly to their avatars, and sessions were recorded so that patients could listen to them at home for further learning reinforcement.

A one-year-long randomised trial that compared virtual reality-assisted therapy to CBT for patients with treatment-resistant schizophrenia highlights the potential of VR to enhance traditional therapy. In this study, manualised and rigorously controlled therapies were implemented for a particularly difficult-to-treat patient population (Dellazizzo et al., 2021). VR-assisted therapy involved 7–9 sessions where patients were immersed in virtual environments and encouraged to speak to personalised avatars that mimicked the abusive, hostile and critical voices patients experienced. These encounters provoked strong negative emotions in patients. Therapists encouraged patients to manage emotions with coping skills and to assertively express themselves to the voices. As VR-assisted therapy progressed, the voices became less hostile, which empowered patients to continue to assert themselves and build self-esteem.

CBT in this study began with assessment and psychoeducation regarding hallucinations. Voices were conceptualised as triggers instead of beliefs, and patients completed voice journals to track their hallucinations and understand their triggers. As CBT progressed, patients identified beliefs that caused distress related to the voices, learned to interpret situations more realistically, practised mindfulness and posited alternate explanations to replace their beliefs about the voices. The results of this study indicated that both interventions were effective and led to clinically meaningful improvements in symptoms. However, VRT was associated with larger effects on overall AVH, distress and frequency; these effects were maintained at a one-year follow-up. VRT significantly reduced persecutory beliefs associated with AVH, and patients who completed VRT engaged more with their voices.

These findings emphasise the importance of experiential interventions that enable patients to directly confront distressing voices, which allows them to test and modify the beliefs they hold about the voices. Additionally, clinician-rated anxiety and depression levels were significantly lower for VRT patients, which is likely to be due to the emphasis in VRT on confronting and experiencing painful or distressing emotions. Virtual encounters elicited strong emotions, which patients learned to regulate without avoidance or safety behaviours. This may lead to decreased avoidance and withdrawal and increased empowerment, which can reduce anxiety and depression and increase overall quality of life. Dellazizzo and colleagues concluded that VR therapy is a promising treatment because it triggers strong emotions, facilitates emotion regulation without avoidance or safety behaviours and improves self-image. The experiential nature of these interventions helps consolidate the learning that occurs during sessions, making it more likely that in-session gains will translate to improved functioning in daily life.

Executive Functioning Deficits

The primary symptoms of psychosis – disorganised thinking, speech and behaviour – all worsen executive functioning. Executive functions are the cognitive processes that allow people to make decisions, plan for the future, carry out complex tasks and display self-control. Treatment with medication and psychotherapy often reduces the positive symptoms of psychosis; however, if executive functioning deficits are not addressed, negative symptoms and functional impairment persist.

People with psychotic disorders often have difficulty engaging socially, performing routine activities of daily living (e.g., making meals, self-care, grocery shopping), or completing work tasks due to executive functioning deficits. The goal of cognitive rehabilitation or re-training is to restore or improve executive functioning through the use of specific interventions tailored to patients' needs. Social cognition therapy often uses role-plays, story vignettes or comic strip tasks to help patients develop theory of mind (the ability to infer the mental state of others) and practise social skills like emotion matching and making conversation. Therapists teach patients to break complex tasks into smaller, more manageable steps, to set realistic and attainable goals and to weigh the pros and cons to facilitate decision-making.

Many patients struggle to find motivation to engage in cognitive rehabilitation, leading to high attrition rates. Moreover, patients have difficulty translating skills gained in therapy sessions to real-life situations. Incorporating VR into cognitive rehabilitation can address these issues (Larson et al., 2014). VR is engaging and acceptable to most patients, and many rehabilitation tasks can be gamified to increase engagement and build motivation. Virtual environments can be tailored to simulate the environments and situations that patients find most challenging, such as stores, restaurants or public transportation. Immersive VR elicits the same thoughts, emotions and behaviours that are triggered when patients interact in their physical reality, but provides a safe space for them to practise new skills, manage distress and drop safety behaviours while the therapist provides encouragement and support.

Adery and colleagues (2018) demonstrated the efficacy of 10 sessions of Multimodal Adaptive Social Intervention in Virtual Reality (MASI-VR) for improving social functioning and outcomes in 16 patients with schizophrenia. Retention rates were high, and most patients reported being extremely satisfied with the intervention. This intervention was associated with significant decreases in clinical symptoms, particularly negative symptoms.

A randomised clinical trial tested the effectiveness of nine 50-minute weekly VR sessions targeting deficits in social cognition in people with psychotic disorders (Vass et al., 2022). The VR sessions focused on improving theory of mind (VR-TOM) through interaction with avatars. When compared to patients who completed the same number of passive VR sessions, patients in the VR-TOM intervention group showed significant improvements in negative symptoms and theory of mind. This study demonstrates one way that VR can successfully reduce executive functioning deficits and suggests that improved executive functioning leads to reduced symptomatology, particularly for negative symptoms. A further benefit was that the VR technology was well-tolerated by the participants in this study.

The research described in the previous sections has shown that VR can enhance treatment outcomes for psychotic disorders. Virtual exposures enable patients with persecutory delusions to test their beliefs and engage in interactions with others in a safe environment. Patients with auditory hallucinations can confront and challenge their voices, which enhances recovery by lowering the distress triggered by the voices and build resilience. Furthermore, VR can help patients practise social skills, reduce executive functioning deficits and learn important self-care skills.

Case Example: Peter

Peter is a 35-year-old man with a diagnosis of schizophrenia. He experiences auditory hallucinations, paranoia, social isolation and disorganised thinking. He completed high school but has been unemployed most of his adult life due to his psychotic symptoms. He lives with his brother and has minimal social interaction. Peter's brother found a therapist who specialises in using virtual reality to enhance cognitive behavioural therapy for psychosis, and Peter has agreed to begin treatment.

The initial phase of therapy involves psychoeducation and cue-desensitisation exposure therapy. Peter's therapist uses virtual reality to create immersive environments specifically designed to trigger Peter's paranoia and avoidance. During these sessions, Peter is instructed to walk through various environments (e.g., restaurants, grocery stores, public transportation) and verbalise his paranoid thoughts. The environments are adjusted based on his feedback. His therapist works with him to challenge these thoughts and encourages Peter to resist avoidance and other safety behaviours.

After four virtual reality sessions, Peter is able to sit with the distress triggered by exposure to virtual public places and start to work on methods to challenge his paranoid thoughts. His therapist uses AVATAR therapy to target Peter's auditory hallucinations. Peter and his therapist work together to create an avatar that resembles the source of the voices that most trouble Peter. Peter's avatar resembles a demon with dark hair and burning eyes. During AVATAR therapy, Peter virtually encounters this "demon" as it taunts him. Peter argues back against what the avatar is saying and counters with truths about himself. As therapy progresses, the avatar begins to respond to Peter less aggressively, which empowers him to further confront and expose the voices as inaccurate and manageable.

Following these two interventions, Peter is better able to function in public places and is no longer distressed by the voices he occasionally experiences. However, he continues to struggle with disorganised thinking and social anxiety from his years of isolation. His therapist uses virtual reality to help Peter improve his executive functioning by practising everyday tasks like personal hygiene, cooking simple meals and using public transportation. As Peter begins to feel more competent with these tasks, his therapist uses VR-based social skills training to strengthen Peter's ability to connect with others and form meaningful relationships.

Depression

People suffering from depression experience depressed mood and/or loss of interest or pleasure, along with at least four of the following symptoms: changes in appetite, insomnia or hypersomnia, psychomotor retardation or agitation, fatigue or diminished energy, feelings of worthlessness or excessive guilt, difficulties in concentration or decision-making and recurrent thoughts of death or suicidal ideation. These symptoms must be present nearly every day for at least two weeks and cause significant impairment in relationships, work/school or other important daily activities (American Psychiatric Association, 2013).

CBT is one of the empirically supported treatments for depression. The cognitive component of CBT for depression addresses the pervasive and distorted patterns of thought associated with depression. Examples of distorted thought patterns include catastrophising, overgeneralisation, personalisation, black-and-white thinking and mind-reading. These maladaptive patterns maintain depression by increasing negative affect, which leads to increased isolation and withdrawal, further limiting opportunities to experience joy or pleasure, which increases depressed mood and so on. CBT therapists teach patients about these distortions, help them identify the distortions colouring their thoughts and train them to evaluate, challenge and ultimately replace them with more adaptive thoughts.

The behavioural component of CBT for depression centres on *behavioural activation*. When people are depressed, they often withdraw from the world and become isolated. Isolation worsens depression by removing opportunities to experience joy or pleasure. Behavioural activation teaches patients to identify how their behaviour impacts their thoughts and feelings. Patients are asked to keep an activity log to track their mood before and after engaging in various activities. Patients are encouraged to schedule and complete activities (e.g., taking a nature walk, meeting a friend for coffee, taking a bath) and to track these activities on their log. As therapy progresses, patients begin to identify activities that boost their mood and are encouraged to increase engagement in activities that generate pleasure, meaning or accomplishment.

Behavioural activation also enables patients to test their distorted beliefs. A patient who believes herself incapable of enjoying anything may experience a small boost in mood by noticing the beauty of nature on a walk. Someone who believes that other people do not enjoy their company may be surprised by the warm reception of a friend when meeting for coffee. VR could be used as a form of behavioural activation for people suffering from depression, particularly early in treatment when low mood and anhedonia make it challenging to motivate clients to engage in activities. VR can be used to create personalised exposure environments designed to boost mood.

Additionally, VR games can build motivation by rewarding activity and engagement, which may then prompt the individual to engage in activities outside the virtual world.

VR could also be used to create immersive experiences for cognitive restructuring. Imagine a virtual environment where a patient can interact with various alternative thoughts and select one to replace a negative automatic thought. Patients are often instructed to visualise throwing negative thoughts away or watching them pass by as clouds; with VR, they could experience this in an interactive, immersive environment. Perhaps the multisensory nature of these experiences could solidify the learning taking place and increase the likelihood that this learning would translate into improved functioning in the physical world.

Research investigating the value of adding VR to CBT for depression is limited, but there are several ways that this technology can be used to target depression. Depression can cause people to focus only on the negative aspects of events while disregarding or overlooking anything positive. One study used VR to help participants with depression improve their mood and increase their ability to create vivid memories of positive experiences (Chen et al., 2021). Participants completed 13 sessions of immersion in a positive virtual environment. After each session, they were instructed to write a description of the VR scene that identified the most positive aspect of the experience and any positive emotions or sensations they experienced during the immersion. This study found significant decreases in self-reported anhedonia, depression, anxiety and functional impairment between baseline and the one-month follow-up.

Another study used VR to enhance behavioural activation (Colombo et al., 2022). Participants with moderate to moderately severe depression completed four virtual reality-based sessions that asked them to select a place and activity (like walking through Paris) to complete in a virtual environment. In this study, VR behavioural activation led to increases in activity levels and decreases in depression symptoms. Similarly, Shah and colleagues (2015) used three daily one-hour sessions consisting of psychoeducation and a VR relaxation exercise and found significant decreases in subjective stress, depression and anxiety and increased relaxation.

While research is still emerging, there are several avenues by which VR could be used to enhance psychotherapy for depression. Engaging and pleasant virtual environments can be used to distract from negative thoughts or to boost mood. Enjoyable virtual activities and games can improve mood and increase motivation to engage in real-world activities that provide opportunities for positive experiences that challenge negative beliefs. Interactive and multisensory virtual exercises requiring patients to throw out negative automatic thoughts and replace them with more accurate and helpful thoughts could solidify new learning and improve mood.

Conclusion

VR can enhance cognitive interventions for a variety of mental health conditions. The immersive nature of VR makes it a powerful distraction technique for people experiencing acute or chronic pain, psychotic symptoms or negative mood. Virtual environments can be specifically tailored to confront and challenge patients' negative or maladaptive beliefs, leading to decreased withdrawal and isolation. Symptoms that are notoriously difficult to treat, like distorted body image and body dissatisfaction in eating disorders and auditory hallucinations in psychotic disorders, can be effectively addressed through embodied, multisensory virtual interventions designed to shift patients' beliefs, strengthen their sense of self and improve their quality of life. For depression, VR can boost mood, help patients re-engage in enjoyable activities and learn to challenge and replace negative or unhelpful thoughts.

9

Skills Training

Introduction

In addition to exposure therapy and cognitive retraining, cognitive behavioural therapy (CBT) often includes a skills training component. For example, a patient with agoraphobia may have lost social skills due to being confined for years, and therapy could include social skills training with role-playing. Patients who have withdrawn and isolated over prolonged episodes of depression may need assistance identifying and pursuing new hobbies or leisure activities.

However, some mental health concerns require more specific and intense skills training. This section describes how VR can enhance social skills training for people with autism spectrum disorders (ASD) and refusal skills training for people receiving treatment for substance use disorders. This section also discusses the application of VR for training in emotion regulation skills that improve well-being across the spectrum of mental health concerns.

Social Skills for Autism

ASD is characterised by persistent impairments in social communication and social interaction that occur in several contexts. Examples of these impairments include difficulties with understanding and reciprocating emotional expressions, difficulty perceiving and understanding non-verbal or social cues and difficulty engaging and maintaining relationships with others. Behaviour patterns in individuals with ASD may include stereotyped or repetitive movements, inflexibility, fixed routines, intense, but narrow interests and adverse or unusual responses to sensory input. To capture the dimensional nature of the deficits associated with ASD, DSM-5 includes three severity levels: Level 1 (requires support), Level 2 (requires substantial support) and Level 3 (requires very substantial support) (American Psychiatric Association, 2013).

DOI: 10.1201/b23370-11

Social skills deficits are one of the primary targets of therapy for ASD. Many people with ASD have average or above-average intellectual capabilities and desire close relationships. Social skills deficits cause many problems with school and work and put people at risk for loneliness, isolation and reduced quality of life. Social skills training (SST) is a well-established component of treatment for people with ASD. SST involves helping patients recognise and reciprocate emotional expression, maintain appropriate eye contact, initiate and maintain conversation and cooperate with others. Traditional SST uses rote instruction, role-plays, storyboards, group therapy and other activities to help patients build the skills that provide the foundation for making and maintaining meaningful relationships.

Incorporating VR into social skills training can increase the ecological validity of the intervention, make patients more motivated to participate fully in training and improve the generalisability of skills to real-world situations. VR SST involves immersing patients in virtual settings that closely resemble situations they encounter in their everyday lives, making the training more realistic. Virtual settings can be modified to include specific locations or situations that are particularly difficult or distressing for a specific patient, including:

- Classrooms
- Restaurants
- Shops
- Parties at other people's homes
- Public transportation
- Air travel
- Job interviews
- School lunchrooms
- Playgrounds

The immersive nature of these interventions blocks distractions from the physical world and increases focus on the task at hand. Multisensory interactive experiences create deeper levels of learning and retention, making it more likely that the skills practised will generalise to real-world behaviour. Additionally, many people with ASD find technology and computers highly motivating and enjoyable, meaning that a more effective intervention can be offered in a manner that feels pleasurable and rewarding, which is likely to increase engagement and improve outcomes.

Research has shown that VR has exciting potential for augmenting social skills training for people with ASD. One study employed VR to create a dynamic facial recognition task to compare the performance of teenagers with ASD and age-matched controls (Bekele et al., 2014). Participants viewed avatars displaying various facial expressions associated with specific emotions and were asked to identify the emotion displayed, rate the level of intensity of that emotion and rate their confidence in their choices. The VR software included eye tracking to analyse participants' gaze during facial information processing. Results showed similar accuracy across groups for accurately identifying emotions and emotional intensity, but revealed that teenagers with ASD reported lower confidence in their ratings and diminished variability in gaze patterns. Consequently, repeated practice with VR tasks could build confidence, reduce social anxiety and increase social engagement.

Studies have also investigated the impact of VR-based social skills interventions for children and young adults with ASD. One small study examined the effectiveness of a VR intervention aimed at increasing social understanding and skills in three children with ASD and found that non-verbal communication, social initiation and social cognition improved over the six weeks of the intervention (Cheng et al., 2015).

Using VR to gamify social skills interventions is another promising treatment avenue for ASD. Craig and colleagues (2016) used an interactive VR game for elementary-aged children that incorporates social-emotional learning strategies into a virtual environment. The virtual environments can be tailored specifically to each child's needs and require the child to navigate social problem-solving tasks. Compared to a waitlist control group, children who completed this intervention exhibited enhanced impulse control, emotion regulation, social initiation and more adaptive social behaviour. Additionally, children reported significant improvements in social self-efficacy, social satisfaction and higher social literacy following the intervention. This study demonstrates the utility of a game-based VR approach to social skills training for children with ASD.

Similarly, Ke and Moon (2018) employed OpenSimulator, which is an immersive virtual playground environment that allows for competition-themed gaming, role-playing and architectural gaming. In this study, this VR-based gaming system effectively promoted social interaction in eight 10–14-year-old youths with high-functioning autism. Rosenfield and colleagues (2019) highlighted the importance of safe, virtual environments for children and teenagers with ASD to practise social interactions without the pressures of real life or the potential negative consequences of making social mistakes in the physical world. These researchers created a virtual environment called Bob's Fish Shop that allows users to practise social interactions; hardware tracks users' gaze, the length of time it takes users to respond to Bob and the verbal interactions between Bob and the user. Information gathered from these VR systems can be used to provide coaching and feedback in a safe and controlled environment, which can decrease social anxiety in people with ASD. Repeated practice in safe environments can help patients generalise these skills to a variety of real-world settings, increase their social self-efficacy and enhance their quality of life by opening new possibilities in relationships and social interactions.

Several studies support the efficacy of Virtual Reality Social Cognition Training (VR-SCT) (Kandalaft et al., 2013; Didehbani et al., 2016) for children and young adults with ASD. VR-SCT is designed for users of various ages, and the characteristics and complexity of numerous social scenarios can be adjusted to fit the age/developmental level. In VR-SCT, users practise social interactions in a variety of virtual contexts while trained clinicians provide coaching and support. This creates a safe environment for people with ASD to practise anxiety-provoking or difficult social interactions while receiving real-time feedback from their therapists. In many sessions, a patient and a peer enter the virtual environment together, interact with each other and other avatars and benefit from the coaching given to each user by the therapist.

One study investigating VR-SCT found that eight young adults (aged 18–26) who completed ten sessions spanning five weeks demonstrated significant improvements in social cognition measures relating to theory of mind and emotion recognition, as well as improvements in real-life social and occupational functioning (Kandalaft et al., 2013). These findings are important in that they show that gains made in the virtual environment translated to improvements in real-world functioning.

Didehbani and colleagues (2016) tested the efficacy of VR-SCT for young people aged 7–16 with ASD. In this study, participants completed 10 sessions of VR-SCT over five weeks; each session involved 45 minutes of virtual interaction with a peer and avatars, followed by a five-minute discussion with the therapist. VR environments included a classroom, a school lunchroom, a playground, a campground, a racetrack, a fast-food restaurant, a technology store, an apartment, a coffee house, a sports store and a park. Social scenarios involved meeting new people, dealing with a bully, bonding with friends, confronting conflict, consoling a friend or handling difficult social situations like catching someone cheating or meeting a stranger. The results of this study showed that VR-SCT was associated with improved emotion recognition, social attribution and executive function.

It is important to note that the VR-SCT discussed above was not an immersive VR environment. The program used avatars and keyboard controls that were realistic enough to provide a sense of presence and real-time interaction between peers and avatars. These researchers chose this design to prevent users from being overwhelmed by a multisensory immersive experience and explained that people with ASD commonly experience sensory processing deficits that could increase the likelihood of cybersickness from immersive VR. While this may be a valid concern for some patients, other studies using immersive VR have not noted increased rates of cybersickness or negative effects. On the contrary, participants with ASD report high levels of engagement and satisfaction with this technology. Future research should explore the benefits of fully immersive VR-SCT, as it is reasonable to conclude that increased presence, ecological validity and engagement could further enhance the improvements observed in these studies.

Incorporating VR into therapy for ASD provides patients with a safe and customised environment to develop and practise social interactions. The ecological validity of virtual environments is superior to role-playing and skills practice in the therapist's office. It removes the risks inherent in practising these skills in the real world. As such, using VR for SST could lead to greater generalisability of skills to real-world behaviour, enabling more people with ASD to form and maintain close relationships to enhance their quality of life.

Skills Training for Addiction

People in recovery from substance abuse must develop strong refusal skills or risk relapsing. One of the important concepts within the recovery community is the necessity of identifying "people, places and things" that can be triggers for relapse. This means that people in recovery must avoid the people they formerly used substances with, the places where substances are available or used and the objects associated with use. It may be possible for people recovering from street drugs like heroin or methamphetamine to successfully avoid the people and places associated with drugs, but for more socially acceptable or culturally embedded substances like alcohol or marijuana, this can be nearly impossible.

CBT for substance use disorders often includes training in refusal skills. Patients and therapists practise how to refuse substances during group or individual therapy sessions. But, refusing hypothetical drugs offered by a therapist or peer in a clinical setting like a group meeting or a therapist's office is quite different from being offered alcohol or drugs at a party or in a restaurant or bar, particularly when the sights, smells and sounds of the setting have triggered a strong craving. For this reason, refusal skills from therapy often fail to generalise to real-world settings.

VR can be used to overcome the limitations of traditional refusal skills training. Research has demonstrated that virtual environments elicit strong cravings for people with substance use disorders (Wiebe et al., 2022). Using VR, patients can be immersed in environments that closely resemble the settings and situations in which they used substances and can safely practise refusal skills while experiencing cravings. Interactive, multisensory virtual experiences would likely lead to deeper learning and enhanced generalisation of skills to real-world settings.

These experiences could also build the patient's self-efficacy for managing strong cravings without resorting to substance use. Therapists can coach patients in real time to use emotion regulation skills like mindfulness and relaxation training to manage cravings. As patients experience success using these skills to manage cravings, they will begin to feel more confident about their ability to refuse substances and manage cravings or negative emotional experiences outside of therapy, which reduces the risk of relapse.

VR can also be useful for developing other skill sets that are often lacking in people with substance use disorders. For example, substance use disorders are associated with lower rates of employment and increased risk of poverty and homelessness. A study evaluating the efficacy of virtual reality job interview training (VR-JIT) found higher rates of competitive employment after six months (78.6% vs. 44.4%) for participants with substance use disorders who completed ten hours of virtual training compared to those who received treatment as usual (Smith et al., 2016). Additionally, VR-JIT was associated with fewer weeks spent pursuing employment. This is important because unemployment is stressful and can increase the risk of relapse, whereas successful employment can motivate recovery maintenance. Notably, participants in this study reported that the virtual training was acceptable, helpful and enjoyable.

VR can be a valuable tool for helping patients overcome substance use disorders and maintain sobriety. Virtual environments customised to mimic the environments within which patients used specific substances trigger strong cravings, which allow patients to practise using refusal skills and coping strategies during cravings. The skills built during these virtual experiences will empower clients to manage cravings and triggers in the real world without relapsing. VR can also help develop other skills that people with substance use disorders may need, like practising job interviews or other life skills that may have been lost after years of substance abuse.

Case Example: Michael (continued)

After several weeks of VR-based cue desensitisation, Michael reports decreased frequency and intensity of cravings. He has maintained sobriety for eight weeks and has been attending daily Narcotics Anonymous (NA) meetings. Michael has been getting better at recognising the "people, places and things," that were triggers of his substance use.

However, Michael is in a complicated situation, as his co-workers and work-related activities were implicated in his substance use. Michael is unwilling to leave his job. VR-based skills training for addiction can help Michael practise refusal skills in virtual environments that closely resemble the situations in which he has previously consumed alcohol and cocaine. Now that Michael has effective skills for managing negative affect and cravings, he can practise turning down substances in safe, but realistic virtual environments. Because he can be immersed in virtual restaurants, bars and clubs that closely resemble the places he frequents for work, the refusal skills he practises are more likely to generalise to his behaviour outside of therapy.

Emotion Regulation to Improve Well-Being

Emotion regulation is the ability to experience and respond to emotions in healthy and adaptive ways. One key to emotion regulation is understanding that the human experience encompasses the entire emotional spectrum. Experiencing painful and distressing emotions is just as human as experiencing pleasure and joy. Emotional dysregulation is a core feature of many mental health conditions and occurs when emotions are not properly managed. Emotional dysregulation can vary depending on the person and the condition involved, but includes a broad range of reactions, including intense mood swings, self-destructive behaviour, dissociation or avoidance.

The early stages of psychotherapy often involve teaching patients emotion regulation skills, as it is difficult or impossible to engage in behavioural interventions and cognitive restructuring when people are highly dysregulated. For example, psychotherapy for the four case examples (Alex, Olivia, Peter and Michael) would be likely to include training in emotion regulation skills.

Relaxation Training

The autonomic nervous system operates without conscious awareness but is responsible for maintaining and regulating vital processes like breathing rate, heart rate, blood pressure, digestion, muscle tension and more. This system contains two branches, the sympathetic nervous system and the parasympathetic nervous system. These dynamic systems work in tandem; activation of one system inhibits the other. The sympathetic nervous system activates during stress to produce the "fight or flight" response. Increased respiration, heart rate, muscle tension and blood pressure are signals indicating activation of this system, which works to increase oxygen and blood to fuel the brain and muscles during emergencies. The parasympathetic nervous system is the "rest and digest" system responsible for bringing the body back to equilibrium. Activation of this system lowers respiration, heart rate, muscle tension and blood pressure and promotes relaxation.

These systems were well designed to manage the daily survival threats encountered by our ancestors, but are often out of sync with the threats of the modern world. Many hallmarks of modern culture, like the twenty-four-hour news cycle, the technological advancements that created endless workdays, doom scrolling social media, the emphasis on productivity and achievement over well-being and restoration and constant information overload have tricked our autonomic nervous system into a state of chronic overactivation. The goal of relaxation training is to restore balance to these systems by tamping down unnecessary sympathetic nervous system activation through intentional activation of the parasympathetic nervous system.

There are many different techniques for inducing relaxation, including biofeedback training, progressive muscle relaxation, guided imagery and diaphragmatic breathing.

Biofeedback

Relaxation biofeedback training has been shown to reliably decrease everyday stress and anxiety (Palekar et al., 2015; Weerdmeester et al., 2020). Biofeedback training uses sensors to measure physiological indicators of sympathetic nervous system activation, including respiration rate, heart rate, heart rate variability, galvanic skin response, blood pressure and brain waves. During relaxation biofeedback training, individuals engage in relaxation techniques like deep breathing, progressive muscle relaxation and mindfulness, while receiving feedback from physiological sensors. The focus is on using objective physiological indicators to gain control over autonomic nervous system activity. Patients are coached in using the measurements generated as gauges of autonomic activation. Physiological measurements help patients identify effective strategies for controlling breathing and relaxing muscle tension, with concomitant decreases in heart rate and blood pressure and increases in relaxation and positive affect.

Diaphragmatic Breathing

Diaphragmatic breathing is a breathing technique shown to elicit relaxation. The diaphragm is a muscle located under the lungs that contracts and expands automatically during breathing. When inhaling, the diaphragm contracts and moves down, which opens the chest cavity to allow for fuller expansion of the lungs. The diaphragm relaxes and moves up during exhalation, which helps force air out of the lungs. During stress or anxiety, people tend to breathe rapidly and shallowly, which can cause an increase in heart and respiration rates and trigger sympathetic nervous system activation. Diaphragmatic breathing promotes relaxation by focusing attention on the movement of the diaphragm during slow, deep breath cycles. This type of breathing facilitates oxygen exchange and stimulates the vagus nerve, which then activates the parasympathetic nervous system, which restores equilibrium and promotes relaxation (Subbalakshmi et al., 2014).

During diaphragmatic breathing, individuals are instructed to lie flat on their backs or sit up straight in a chair, while placing one hand on the abdomen and the other hand on the chest. Then they are asked to breathe in slowly and deeply so that the hand on the chest remains still while the hand on the abdomen moves out. Exhaling slowly, the hand on the abdomen should move back in towards the body while the hand on the chest remains still. Diaphragmatic breathing is effective in reducing anxiety and negative affect (Chen et al., 2017; Ma et al., 2017) and improving mood and relaxation (Hopper et al., 2019; Perciavalle et al., 2017).

Progressive Muscle Relaxation

Progressive muscle relaxation (PMR) trains people to relax by sequentially flexing and relaxing muscle groups. PMR has been shown to reduce anxiety, increase well-being and improve quality of life (Conrad and Roth, 2007; Li et al., 2020). During PMR, individuals are instructed to flex and hold tension in specific muscle groups for five seconds and then relax, while focusing their attention on the contrasting sensations involved in tension and relaxation. Instructors may advise individuals to visualise the tension draining out of each muscle group as the exercise progresses through the large muscle groups of the body, beginning with the feet, moving up the legs, through the abdomen and core, down the arms to the hands and ending with neck and facial muscles.

Guided Imagery

Guided imagery is a relaxation technique in which individuals visualise peaceful or positive images or scenarios. Some guided imagery techniques involve therapists asking patients to vividly imagine a peaceful place or their favourite travel destination. Therapists guide patients to notice the details of these locations and experiences, highlighting all sensory experiences. Other guided imagery exercises use pre-written scripts describing peaceful locations and experiences. Patients are asked to imagine themselves in these locations as vividly as possible to enhance relaxation.

VR Applications for Relaxation Training

The efficacy and appeal of relaxation techniques can be enhanced by VR. Many people struggle to maintain focus and attention during relaxation exercises. Immersion in a virtual environment increases focus through appealing and relaxing visual and auditory stimuli while preventing distraction from external stimuli. Multisensory VR environments can engage the senses more easily than using one's imagination, which can deepen relaxation. Additionally, individuals sometimes disregard relaxation training as overly simplistic or not credible. Previous research has demonstrated that patients tend to view VR interventions as more credible; using VR for relaxation training may similarly increase the perceived credibility of the intervention.

Rockstroh and colleagues (2021) developed a VR-based respiratory biofeedback game to facilitate diaphragmatic breathing and investigated its impact on diaphragmatic breathing, relaxation, stress and relaxation-related self-efficacy. The VR game uses a head-mounted display for audio and visual elements and a VR hand controller that users set on their abdomens to detect abdominal movements resulting from respiration. Users' success with diaphragmatic breathing is reflected in the visual elements of the virtual environment; active use of diaphragmatic breathing prompts movement through six levels of a visually appealing nature-based environment. Following six sessions of VR-based diaphragmatic breathing, participants experienced increased involvement of the diaphragm in breathing and increased length of breath cycles, which indicates that the program effectively trained diaphragmatic breathing. Post-session relaxation was higher than pre-session relaxation levels and, upon completion of training, users reported significant increases in self-efficacy related to relaxation and rated the program as likable, easy to use and helpful.

Similarly, Jeong and colleagues (2022) created a VR-based relaxation program that provides training in diaphragmatic breathing and PMR. Testing of this program with healthy participants showed that VR-based self-training programs are effective in increasing relaxation. Participants in this study reported particularly large benefits from the VR-based PMR training. Further support for incorporating VR into relaxation training comes from a study comparing a combination of PMR training and therapist-provided guided imagery to PMR training with a personalised VR relaxation exercise (Pardini et al., 2024). This study showed that personalised VR scenarios successfully induce relaxation and decrease anxiety and tension.

VR can also be used to enhance distraction training for pain management; indeed, the applications of VR-based relaxation training are nearly limitless. These interventions could be incorporated into healthcare settings to teach patients how to manage pain or negative emotions like fear and anxiety. These interventions could increase access to care for people who avoid healthcare settings for a variety of reasons and could be implemented without significant risks or high costs.

Mindfulness

Mindfulness refers to the intentional focusing of attention on the present moment by opening yourself to the experiences occurring both within and around you. It is the conscious direction of attention to your thoughts and emotions, as well as to what is going on in the world around you. Mindfulness trains you to observe non-judgmentally, by accepting things as they are without attaching value judgments like *good* or *bad*. This openness to experience enables you to consider multiple perspectives and helps you avoid rigid and inflexible thinking patterns.

Mindfulness is a skill that requires practice, but, like most skills, the more you practise, the more of a habit it becomes. Research has shown that mindfulness training can reduce anxiety and depression and increase positive emotional experiences and well-being (Bajaj et al., 2016; Carson and Langer,

2006). Over the past few decades, mindfulness has been identified as an important component of evidence-based treatment for many mental health conditions. Mindfulness-based treatments like Acceptance and Commitment Therapy (ACT), Dialectical Behaviour Therapy (DBT) and other third-wave psychotherapy movements shift the focus from changing thoughts and emotions to mindfully observing and accepting them.

People experiencing anxiety often have fears about the future, worry about how others perceive them or have difficulty managing uncertainty or ambiguity. By consciously turning the mind from worries over the future or the past and directing attention to what is currently happening, people can ground themselves in the present moment. Similarly, people who are depressed often get stuck in ruminative thinking patterns. They may obsess over past failures or difficulties, leading to feelings of hopelessness about the future. Rigid and distorted beliefs about themselves and the world close the mind to hope and the possibility of change. Mindfulness interrupts these ruminative cycles, bringing the person back to the present moment and leading to more flexible and adaptive thinking patterns.

It is critical to understand that, despite the large number of mindfulness exercises available, mindfulness is a way of being, or a state of mind, to be pursued, not an activity to engage in for a few minutes at a time. Personality factors and temperament can make individuals more or less naturally mindful, but with consistent practice, anyone can become skilled in mindfulness. Building mindfulness takes dedication and commitment, but the rewards may be unparalleled by any other mental health intervention available. A systematic review of mindfulness studies showed significant improvements in self-awareness, emotional awareness, attentional control, inhibition control, emotion regulation and adaptability following mindfulness practices (Mitsea et al., 2023).

Despite the benefits of practising mindfulness, situational or personal distractions can get in the way. VR may increase the effectiveness of mindfulness practices by removing external auditory and visual stimuli. One study immersed users in a peaceful virtual forest with a voice narrating a mindfulness exercise and found significant increases in state mindfulness and positive affect following the exercise (Seabrook et al., 2020). These participants reported using the visual and auditory elements of the virtual environment as attentional anchors to maintain a mindful state.

A systematic review comparing the effects of traditional mindfulness training to VR-based mindfulness training found that virtual training was more effective (Ma et al., 2023). This review showed that more immersive experiences (head-mounted, 3D) were superior to less immersive experiences (computer-generated, 2D). Additionally, VR-based mindfulness training was associated with improvements in positive mood, attention, anxiety, depression, emotion regulation, stress level and sleep quality.

Substantial research has demonstrated that building mindfulness skills is one of the most effective ways to boost psychological health. VR can aid in developing these skills by preventing distractions and teaching people to focus on the present moment via engaging and effective exercises. VR can increase mindfulness for people seeking treatment for mental health conditions or for anyone who would like to improve their psychological well-being more generally.

Increasing Positive Affect

While most emotion regulation strategies focus on managing and reducing negative affect, increasing and savouring positive affective experiences is also important to well-being. The field of positive psychology has demonstrated the importance of examining and understanding the positive aspects of human experience for building resilience and flourishing (Seligman and Csikszentmihalyi, 2000). Bryant (2003) developed the Savouring Beliefs Inventory (SBI) to measure individuals' ability to find pleasure in anticipating future positive events, savour current positive experiences and remember past positive experiences. Scores on the SBI were positively associated with higher optimism, internal locus of control, life satisfaction, self-esteem and the intensity and frequency of happiness, and negatively correlated with neuroticism, guilt, anhedonia, hopelessness and depression (Bryant, 2003). Other studies have demonstrated that savouring is a key mechanism by which people experience happiness from positive events (Jose et al., 2012).

VR can be used to build savouring skills and boost positive affect. For example, Baños and colleagues (2014) designed a system called 'EARTH of well-being' to elicit positive emotions and reinforce the establishment and savouring of autobiographical memories of positive experiences. Volunteers who completed six sessions of this VR program over six weeks reported significantly increased positive mood at the end of each session. Numerous VR programs could be used to generate positive emotional experiences, particularly programs that allow users to travel to locations all over the world and explore them from a first-person perspective. This could be particularly helpful for older individuals for whom travel may be too difficult or for individuals with limited financial resources.

While these programs have been designed to be self-guided, for patients receiving mental health treatment, the therapist's presence would be important for guiding patients through these experiences. Therapists could provide real-time coaching in focusing attention on the positive aspects of the experience, identifying and savouring positive emotions evoked by the immersions and helping patients form and revisit memories of these positive experiences. Real-time support by therapists would be particularly important for patients with depression, anxiety disorders or psychotic disorders who struggle to maintain attention on positive aspects of experience, without worrying about the future or ruminating on the past.

Research has shown that many people enjoy VR experiences. Engaging in immersive virtual exercises involving travel, outdoor activities or revisiting treasured memories is a way to boost positive affect for individuals who suffer from anxiety, depression and other mental health challenges. VR interventions designed to help patients focus on the positive aspects of experiences and savour pleasant memories can help remediate the negative attentional biases and cognitive distortions common to patients with anxiety and depression.

The behavioural activation worksheet in Figure 9.1 is a structured tool designed to assist individuals in alleviating depressive symptoms through the deliberate scheduling of both pleasurable activities and essential tasks. The worksheet includes a rating scale for users to assess their levels of depression, pleasure and achievement before and after each activity, facilitating self-monitoring and reflection on progress. This process allows individuals to focus on enjoyable pursuits to enhance mood and energy levels, while also addressing neglected responsibilities to foster a sense of accomplishment. By balancing fun activities with achievable tasks, one can proactively disrupt the cycle of depression, leading to improved mental health and well-being.

0	1	2	3	4	5
None	Minimal	Mild	Moderate	High	Extreme

Activity & Date:		Depression	Pleasure	Achievement
	Before:	______	______	______
	After:	______	______	______
Activity & Date:				
	Before:	______	______	______
	After:	______	______	______
Activity & Date:				
	Before:	______	______	______
	After:	______	______	______

FIGURE 9.1
Behavioural activation worksheet demonstrates the impact of behavioural activation on mood and sense of achievement.

Conclusion

This chapter highlights the potential of VR to enhance psychotherapy by describing how VR can be incorporated into the cognitive, behavioural and skills training components of CBT for a variety of mental health conditions. In the hands of a skilled therapist, VR can be a powerful tool for clinical change. It is noteworthy that investigations of the efficacy of VR exposure therapy have found that virtual exposures are at least as effective and sometimes more effective than traditional *in vivo* exposure therapy across many disorders. Virtual exposures are not only effective in eliciting distress and habituation but are also viewed by many patients as more credible and preferable when compared to more traditional treatments. This is important because it increases access to effective therapy, as many patients are hesitant or unwilling to engage in exposure therapy despite its documented effectiveness. The fact that VR can remove this obstacle to effective care is significant. Likewise, VR holds tremendous potential for improving cognitive interventions for many of the difficult issues patients face. The results of research investigating the utility of VR for improving outcomes in eating disorders and psychotic disorders are particularly exciting, as these disorders are notoriously difficult to treat and associated with immense suffering and increased morbidity. Several studies have shown how VR can be used to extend psychotherapy from the realm of theory into embodied experience, with concomitant improvements in patient outcomes.

VR can also be useful for increasing engagement in and the effectiveness of various types of skills training. Virtual environments increase the ecological validity of skills training, making it more likely that skills learned in psychotherapy will translate into improvements in everyday functioning. Using VR to enhance training in emotion regulation skills like relaxation training and mindfulness can benefit patients regardless of diagnostic category and lead to meaningful improvements in well-being.

It is important to consider that research investigating VR for psychotherapy has been piecemeal. The case examples provided in this section illustrate how VR can be implemented into multiple components of treatment, which may be particularly important for conditions like eating disorders and psychotic disorders, which can be more difficult to treat. However, current research is limited only to the incorporation of VR into specific components of treatment, like cue-desensitisation or cognitive restructuring, but not into the full therapeutic process. While this is an important first step, it does not capture the gestalt of psychotherapy. Imagine the possibilities when VR is implemented into every step of psychotherapy, including assessment, cognitive training, cue desensitisation, skills training and emotion regulation.

Part 3

Future Directions of Psychotherapy in the Metaverse

The potential for using virtual reality (VR) in psychotherapy coincided with the increased availability of personal computers in the 1990s. For the first time, advancements in computer technology allowed reductions in the size and cost of computers. As personal computers became commonplace in many homes, internet technology connected people across the globe. People began accessing mental health services remotely via the internet, and self-help CBT programs were launched (Carlbring et al., 2001; Spek et al., 2007).

Psychologists began developing VR programs for treating phobias like fear of flying, heights and public speaking (Lamson and Meisner, 1994; Rothbaum et al., 1995). These VR programs allowed clinicians to immerse patients in realistic, multisensory and interactive environments where their fears could be confronted in a safe and highly controllable manner. Clinicians began to realise that virtual technology could transform psychotherapeutic interventions, but the state of technology at that time could not allow this potential to be fully realised.

Slow processing speeds, low refresh rates and primitive graphics yielded less than ideal virtual environments. Head-mounted devices for these systems were cumbersome, heavy and required many wires. Patients and clinicians found these systems difficult to navigate and clunky, which led many to feel disillusioned with this technology. At this point, VR had failed to live up to expectations.

DOI: 10.1201/b23370-12

A notable exception to these failed attempts was the CAVE, or Cave Automatic Virtual Environment, developed by several research institutions during the late 1990s and early 2000s (e.g., Meyerbröker, 2014; Laforest, Bouchard, Bossé and Mesly, 2016). In contrast to head-mounted devices, CAVE is a projection-based VR system in which stereoscopic, computer-generated images are projected onto the walls of a room. Patients wear glasses that adjust dark and light in sync with the projected images. Sensors embedded in the glasses are part of an electromagnetic tracking system that allows the patient to interact with the virtual environment. While these systems have demonstrated efficacy for treating various psychological disorders, the sheer magnitude and cost of the systems are prohibitive.

Drastic progress in computer and information processing during the first two decades of the 21st century catalysed demand for personalised mobile devices, including smartphones, wearable devices and highly realistic gaming systems. Increasing availability of high-speed networks meant that nearly everyone had a personal computer with internet access, high processing speeds, cameras and enhanced graphics in their pockets. These technological advances meant that the promise of VR could reasonably be attained, which revived interest in and development of consumer VR systems.

The previous sections of this book outlined how VR can be incorporated into clinical practice to enhance psychotherapeutic interventions. With the release of numerous commercially available, portable and relatively affordable VR systems, a future in which virtual interventions are a standard component of psychotherapy is easier to envision. This chapter will describe innovations in VR technology that are relevant to clinicians who are interested in the most effective way to implement VR interventions.

It has been several years since Meta CEO Mark Zuckerberg announced that his company's primary focus would shift to developing their own metaverse, a fully immersive virtual platform where people can socialise, receive medical and mental health care and even buy and sell virtual real estate (Cross, 2023). While this virtual platform has yet to be realised, development continues and the innovations discussed in the following sections will impact the experience of psychotherapy in the metaverse.

10

Hardware Improvements

Introduction

The streamlined, elegant VR headsets and controllers currently available for purchase are a far cry from the original head-mounted display revealed by Ivan Sutherland in 1968. Technological advances in the decades that followed have catapulted VR beyond the early systems introduced to the public by gaming companies like Nintendo and Sega in the 1980s and 1990s. The 2010s witnessed the unprecedented motion-tracking technology and visual innovations of headsets released by Oculus and HTC Vive; these products opened the door to new possibilities for virtual technology. Numerous industries, including healthcare, education and engineering, are embracing VR as a powerful tool for training, productivity and intervention.

Advances in visual technology, tracking and input methods and audio innovations have spurred the development of highly immersive and portable VR systems. Consumers, companies and industries are embracing VR in record numbers as access to a fully developed, dynamic and multifaceted metaverse appears imminent. The hardware necessary to access the metaverse is constantly evolving and ever increasing.

Accessing a metaverse requires only a smartphone or tablet. However, to fully immerse yourself and experience the metaverse the way it was designed to be experienced, you will need a powerful laptop or desktop computer containing a good graphics card, a fast processor and a strong internet connection. You will also need a high-resolution VR headset. Hardware options vary widely in appearance, comfort and quality. In general, however, the higher the quality of your hardware, the better the virtual experience.

The characteristics of the hardware used to access the metaverse influence the experience of the metaverse; therefore, the decision about which hardware to purchase can directly impact the experience of virtual psychotherapy. Consequently, carefully considering these options is crucial, as they can directly influence your patients' experience and may alter the effectiveness of virtual psychotherapeutic interventions. The following sections will

DOI: 10.1201/b23370-13

describe recent hardware innovations and their potential impact on virtual psychotherapy.

Display and Visual Enhancements

The metaverse is primarily a visual medium, so the better the visual display, the better the virtual experience. While VR requires only a smartphone, the increased resolution and refresh rates of specialised VR headsets produce crisper, clearer visual displays that closely mimic reality. Resolution describes the number of pixels per inch (PPI); higher resolution indicates higher pixel density, which produces sharper images. Refresh rates refer to the number of times the display updates with new images per second. Higher refresh rates create fluid visual displays where movement is smooth and seamless.

While smartphones can be converted into VR goggles, the virtual experience will be less realistic and immersive due to much lower resolution and refresh rates. The iPhone 15, for example, has a resolution of about 460 PPI and a refresh rate of 60 Hz, which is considered the bare minimum refresh rate for VR. A smooth VR experience requires a refresh rate of at least 90 Hz. In contrast, the Meta Quest 2 and the HTC Vive Pro 2 are among the most popular commercially available VR systems, boasting resolutions of 773 PPI (Meta Quest 2) and 950 PPI (HTC Vive Pro 2), with both systems showing refresh rates of up to 120 Hz (Andronico, 2024; Greenwald, 2024).

Field of view (FOV) is another important aspect that affects the visual experience of VR environments. FOV is measured in degrees and refers to the width of the observable world that users can see at any given point. Higher FOV allows users to see more of the world at once without having to move their head. The HTC Vive Pro 2 generates a FOV of 120°, while the Meta Quest 2 produces a 100° FOV.

Technological advances that have improved screen resolution, refresh rates and field of view generate virtual environments that are more seamless and realistic. As a result, users feel a stronger sense of presence in these virtual environments, which can enhance outcomes for virtual psychotherapeutic interventions. Additionally, these improvements make interactions within and movement through the virtual world smooth and fluid, which reduces the likelihood of cybersickness.

The quality of the visual display is important to many virtual psychotherapeutic interventions. Effective exposure therapy for anxiety disorders, OCD and PTSD requires that the exposure environment elicit distressing emotions like fear, anxiety and disgust. High-resolution visual displays can more closely simulate reality to create a more immersive exposure environment. Additionally, visual displays with higher refresh rates and wider FOV may lead to better treatment outcomes for social skills training, refusal skills training or other interventions that enable patients to rehearse skills in the safety of a virtual world.

Tracking and Input Methods

Advances in VR tracking technology have catalysed a shift from outside–in tracking to inside–out tracking. Tracking refers to how the VR system locates the user in 3D space. Initially, VR systems utilised outside–in tracking in which external sensors, typically located on a base station, track the movement and position of markers/sensors attached to the user or the VR devices. External sensors provide reference points in space, and triangulation of data from multiple sensors enables precise calculation of the user's position and orientation.

However, the Oculus Quest revolutionised VR tracking by introducing inside–out tracking using cameras and infrared sensors embedded in the headset and controllers to capture data from the surrounding environment. Tracking algorithms synthesise this data to determine the user's position and movement relative to objects in the environment. Inside–out tracking is simpler and more cost-effective than outside–in tracking because it eliminates the need for external sensors and the associated infrastructure required for processing data from those sensors. Inside–out tracking involves a system contained within the headset and two controllers, making the VR system more streamlined, easier to set up and use and more portable.

Outside–in tracking is associated with higher precision and accuracy, but many users prefer the easier setup and enhanced portability of systems with inside–out tracking. While the HTC Vive Pro 2 requires a base station and uses outside–in tracking, accessories like the Vive Tracker 3.0 can be worn by users to incorporate inside–out tracking as well and to capture full-body movements with incredible accuracy. The availability of these trackers and the number of new VR systems using only inside–out tracking suggest that inside–out tracking will become the standard. Table 10.1 summarises the advantages and disadvantages of each tracking type.

VR systems with inside–out tracking offer several advantages for psychotherapy. Because there are no base stations or external sensors, these systems are easier to set up and can be used efficiently in multiple locations. These advantages may help remove some of the barriers preventing mental health practitioners from incorporating VR into clinical practice. Additionally, patients of clinicians using VR for remote psychotherapy may be more inclined to utilise this technology if very little set-up is required and the VR system can be easily used by others in their family, in various locations around the home and without extensive set-up.

TABLE 10.1

Summary of tracking type with description, advantages and disadvantages

Tracking Type	Description	Advantages	Disadvantages
Outside–in	External sensors located on a base station track users' movement and position	• Higher accuracy • Higher precision	• Requires a base station • More difficult to set up • Decreased portability
Inside–out	Cameras and infrared sensors embedded in the headset and controllers capture data from the environment to determine users' movement and position	• Eliminates the need for a base station • VR system is contained within the headset and controllers • Easier to set up • Easier to operate • Increased portability • More cost-effective	• Lower accuracy • Lower precision

Hand Tracking

Hand tracking is another aspect of VR that continues to evolve. Hand tracking allows interaction with the virtual world without controllers. The capability to manually manipulate objects within virtual environments without using controllers makes virtual experiences feel more natural by removing a physical barrier (the controller) between the user and the environment. Hand tracking is a recent development within the VR world. In 2021, only four out of nineteen VR systems that entered the market included hand tracking. However, by 2022, seven of fifteen new systems supported hand tracking, including HTC Vive XR Elite, Meta Quest Pro, Pico 4 Enterprise and Lynx R1, which indicates that hand tracking is becoming standard for emerging VR systems.

Many VR psychotherapeutic interventions involve the patient manipulating objects within a virtual environment. Any innovation that removes barriers between the patient and the virtual environment is likely to result in a stronger sense of presence within that environment. Hand tracking allows patients to interact with virtual objects more naturally than using controllers, which increases patients' sense of presence in virtual environments and can improve therapy outcomes.

Imagine the enhanced realism and efficacy of a VR intervention for treating arachnophobia if the patient could reach out and touch a virtual spider, rather than using a controller to simulate the action. This tactile interaction could significantly improve the immersion and impact of the exposure therapy. Similarly, consider the profound difference in virtual exposure therapy for a patient with germ-related OCD, where hand tracking technology allows the patient to physically reach out, touch and turn the doorknob or flush the toilet in a filthy public bathroom. This approach contrasts sharply with scenarios where the patient must use a controller to interact with the virtual environment, offering a more authentic and engaging experience.

Patients with psychotic disorders or autism spectrum disorders can also benefit greatly from hand tracking technology in VR therapy. Practising essential skills such as grocery shopping, personal grooming or cooking in a virtual environment that closely mimics real life can significantly enhance the generalisability of these learned skills. The use of hand tracking technology allows for a more natural and intuitive interaction within the virtual space, making the therapeutic exercises more relevant and effective. This advance in VR technology holds great promise for improving the quality and outcomes of psychotherapeutic interventions by creating more realistic, interactive and engaging therapeutic experiences.

Haptic Feedback

Haptic feedback devices provide on-demand physical sensations to users, including vibrations, pressure and temperature. Haptic feedback not only enhances the sense of touch but also increases the realism of the virtual environment. This sensory feedback delivered by haptic devices aligns with the visual and audio content of the virtual environment to produce a stronger sense of immersion and presence. Haptic gloves allow the user to experience the physical sensations associated with touch while immersed in the virtual world. Force feedback simulates the feeling of an object's size and density and is generated by magnetic friction brakes embedded into the gloves. Actuators in the glove fingers simulate the feelings of touching a surface or pushing a button. Haptic gloves may also generate heat or cold sensations associated with the temperature of the virtual environment (Carter, 2024).

Incorporating haptic feedback into psychotherapy in the metaverse can increase the impact of therapeutic interventions. Haptic feedback heightens the realism of the virtual environment, leading to a stronger sense of presence, which has been shown to enhance the effectiveness of psychotherapeutic interventions. Appropriate use of haptic feedback can assist with pain management and relaxation training by providing calming vibrations or by using conditioned sensations as signals to initiate relaxation exercises. Haptic feedback can be especially useful during exposure therapy because more realistic virtual environments will provoke stronger emotional and physiological responses, leading to stronger inhibitory learning and greater self-efficacy.

Audio Innovations

While the visual elements of a virtual environment may be more immediately apparent, the audio components play a critical role in creating realistic and immersive environments. Effective VR requires 3D audio in which sounds are spatially located within the virtual environment. Additionally, the audio environment must be dynamic and responsive to the user's movements and interactions within the virtual environment. As users navigate virtual environments, the sounds they hear must align with their visual experience to maintain a sense of presence and immersion.

Ambisonics is an audio innovation that uses a spherical coordinate system to capture and reproduce sound in 3D space. Unlike television and movies, which project sound in two dimensions, the sounds within a virtual environment must mimic how sound waves interact with objects, or the audio experience will sound unnatural. Many VR systems implement binaural audio systems that use two microphones to simulate natural interaction between sound waves and human ears. Binaural audio enables users to perceive direction and distance in real time, corresponding to the user's movements and position within the environment.

VR psychotherapy can be improved by incorporating high-quality audio technology. This may be particularly important for virtual exposure therapy, whether the patient is immersed in a virtual combat zone to treat PTSD or flying in a virtual plane to treat a fear of flying. VR systems without high-quality audio technology produce virtual experiences that are less realistic, which can reduce the effectiveness of psychotherapeutic interventions by decreasing patients' sense of presence within the virtual environment.

Portability and Comfort

Many of the hardware improvements discussed above have led to VR systems that are more portable and comfortable. For example, inside–out tracking removes the need for external sensors, so systems that use this type of tracking are highly portable. The Meta Quest 2 and 3 involve only a headset and two controllers, allowing for easy transport to a new location and a setup time of less than one minute. Moreover, their cord-free design eliminates the risk of tripping over cables, enhancing both convenience and safety.

As more businesses and consumers embrace VR technology, comfort has emerged as a critical consideration. This trend has driven the development of lighter headsets that can be comfortably worn for extended periods on a variety of diverse face shapes. Adjustable straps and soft foam cushioning are now standard features, further enhancing user comfort. For instance, the Meta Quest 3 weighs just over one pound (515 g), exemplifying the industry's commitment to ergonomic design.

When choosing a VR system for psychotherapy, factors such as portability and comfort must be considered. Opting for a system with inside–out tracking facilitates seamless transitions between therapy sessions and minimises logistical hassles. Additionally, prioritising patient comfort is essential to ensuring effective therapy outcomes. Heavy, uncomfortable headsets can detract from the therapeutic experience, compromising the patient's sense of immersion and engagement.

In therapeutic contexts requiring prolonged VR use, such as interventions like prolonged exposure therapy, headset comfort becomes even more crucial. Patients must feel at ease wearing the headset and holding the controllers for extended periods, as discomfort could detract from therapy effectiveness. Thus, selecting a VR system that balances portability with ergonomic comfort is essential for optimising therapeutic outcomes and patient experience alike.

Conclusion

Hardware plays an important role in the experience and evolution of VR technology. Advancements in visual, tracking, haptic and audio technology have been critical in making VR more appealing to the public. Cumbersome, prohibitively expensive, difficult-to-setup systems have been replaced by streamlined, portable, lightweight headsets and controllers that offer highly realistic, immersive experiences. The field of VR is dynamic and constantly evolving, which means that exciting innovations remain on the horizon.

Due to the hardware advances discussed in this section, the future is full of exciting possibilities for incorporating VR into psychotherapy. However, embracing this technology will require active involvement and collaboration among mental health professionals to ensure that VR is used effectively and ethically. To begin, there should be a standardised set of minimum hardware requirements for effective virtual psychotherapy and clear explanations of how the various hardware options can impact the therapeutic process. This section is an attempt to begin this conversation. Moreover, as much as possible, psychotherapy in the metaverse should mirror in-person psychotherapy in terms of level of presence and comfort. For instance, the hardware used to access the metaverse in psychotherapy should create an immersive therapeutic environment, allowing therapists and clients to feel a stronger sense of connection. A proper VR headset helps promote engagement, reduces distractions and fosters relaxation and safety in a therapeutic setting.

11

Software Improvements

Introduction

Innovations in VR software can unlock the full potential of VR as a powerful tool for enhancing psychotherapeutic interventions. Software improvements that could profoundly improve virtual psychotherapy include the creation of dynamic environments, AI-based cue generation and the inclusion of biofeedback sensors into VR systems. The incorporation of real-time feedback mechanisms would allow therapists to adjust sessions dynamically, ensuring that the therapy remains relevant and effective. These improvements could generate more immersive, interactive and realistic virtual environments to increase patient engagement and improve outcomes across a range of mental health concerns.

Dynamic Environments

In VR, dynamic environments are virtual environments that constantly change and adapt based on the user's experience. Appropriate utilisation of dynamic environments is a crucial next step for VR in psychotherapy. Dynamic environments offer a unique and responsive experience to each individual and adapt alongside each patient's therapeutic journey. These environments can simulate various scenarios that evolve with the patient's progress, ensuring that the therapy remains appropriate and challenging. Dynamic environments that are most beneficial for psychotherapy in a VR environment include adaptive scenarios, interactive objects and real-time feedback based on decision-making. By integrating these elements, therapists can create highly personalised and engaging therapeutic experiences that can significantly enhance treatment outcomes.

DOI: 10.1201/b23370-14

A dynamic environment involving adaptive scenarios can adjust treatment level and intensity based on an individual's progress. For example, an individual being treated for an anxiety disorder in a VR psychotherapy setting can experience various levels of anxiety-inducing stimuli based on their tolerance and progress. This allows virtual exposure therapy to progress in a graduated manner. An individual progressing through treatment for public speaking phobia may begin with virtual exposure environments populated with a small crowd of peers with pleasant facial expressions. As habituation to initial exposure environments occurs, a dynamic virtual environment could shift to a larger crowd populated with older, professional people who are scowling. Artificial intelligence (AI) software could consider the patient's current environment and make recommendations to the therapist for environmental adjustments to make it more challenging. These dynamic environments allow individualised and graduated exposure therapy based on each patient's specific symptoms and treatment progress.

Interactive objects in a VR psychotherapy setting can respond to the individual's actions throughout the session. For example, an individual completing anger management therapy in a VR environment can interact with virtual objects that allow them to physically express and explore their emotions in a controlled, therapeutic setting. Alternatively, patients with OCD would be able to hold and manipulate items, such as soiled clothing or rotten food, as they progress through virtual exposure and response prevention therapy.

In terms of real-time feedback in a psychotherapy VR environment, dynamic environments allow individuals to observe the consequences of particular actions or behaviours. For example, in a VR psychotherapy session focused on improving social skills, an individual can receive immediate feedback regarding nonverbal cues or conversational skills. Avatars populating the virtual environment can react dynamically to the patient's behaviour, providing critical feedback to guide patient learning. This strengthens learning by enabling the patient and therapist to process and discuss behaviours and consequences in real-time. It also makes the virtual experiences more similar to experiences in the real world, which facilitates the transfer of learning from the virtual world to the real world.

The creation of psychotherapy-specific dynamic environments remains a significant barrier to the adoption of VR into clinical practice. While several companies (e.g., XRHealth, PsyTech VR, C2Care) have created interactive virtual environments specifically for psychotherapy, most of these remain relatively standardised and are not fully adaptive or dynamic to specific patient behaviour. Realising the full potential of VR psychotherapy will depend on continued innovation and development of dynamic virtual environments.

AI-Based Cue Generation

Continued innovations in AI will facilitate the development of dynamic and interactive virtual environments. AI can generate personalised virtual content and dynamically modify virtual environments to suit individual preferences and needs. Improvements in AI-based object recognition can create more immersive and interactive virtual experiences by enabling virtual characters (avatars) to recognise and respond to users' movements, facial expressions and physical gestures. Additionally, language processing algorithms can equip avatars to respond to users' questions or commands more naturally and intuitively, further heightening the realism of virtual encounters (Crockett, 2023).

AI can be a powerful tool to create more immersive and interactive virtual psychotherapy environments. Advances in AI will likely lead to emotional intelligence algorithms that allow virtual characters to respond in real-time to patients' emotional states. This can make social encounters within virtual psychotherapy environments feel more authentic. These innovations will lead to virtual psychotherapy interventions that are more engaging and impactful, which will therefore be more likely to improve outcomes for patients with a broad range of mental health concerns.

AI also has potential for creating individualised virtual environments for psychotherapy based on specific patient needs. Patient history, current symptoms and previous treatment experiences could be used by AI to suggest or generate customised VR experiences for patients, which would reduce the burden on mental health professionals.

Biofeedback

Appropriate biofeedback sensors in VR can add great value to the therapeutic experience. Biofeedback is used to build patients' awareness of their physiological functions in real time using sensors that capture physiological data, such as heart rate, skin conductance and brainwave activity. This data not only helps patients understand how their thoughts and emotions impact their physiology but also provides therapists with objective measurements reflecting their patients' emotional states during therapy sessions. This real-time information is invaluable to understanding how the client is reacting to and progressing through the therapeutic process, which enables better treatment planning and enhances treatment outcomes.

Biofeedback can also be useful for creating more dynamic and interactive virtual environments. The data captured by biofeedback sensors can provide feedback that the VR system uses to adjust the virtual environment based on

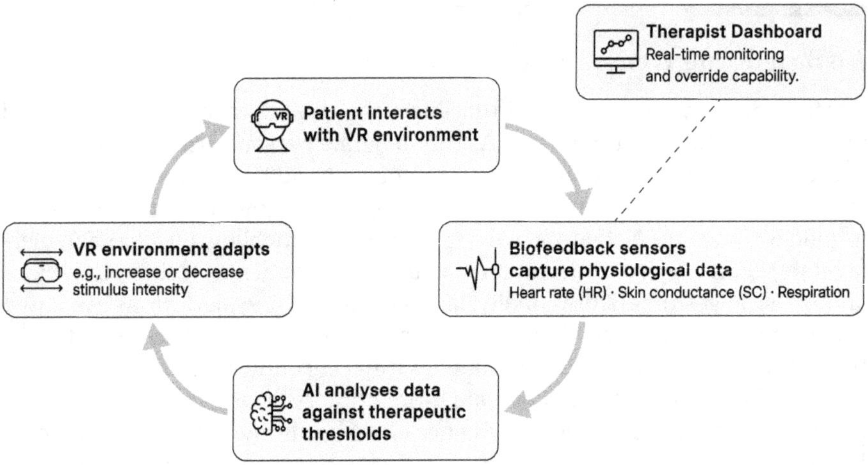

FIGURE 11.1
Biofeedback-driven dynamic environment loop.

therapy goals (see Figure 11.1). Kritikos and colleagues (2021) presented a VR system capable of adjusting virtual exposure environments for arachnophobia (spider phobia) based on variations in skin conductance captured by biofeedback sensors. Various aspects of the virtual exposure environment, including the number of spiders, size of spiders, height of spiders' jumps, spider movement towards the patient and speed of spider movements, were calibrated based on skin conductance to ensure that the patient remained in a heightened emotional state.

Using biofeedback data to adjust virtual environments in real-time is particularly helpful for exposure therapy, but could also strengthen psychological interventions for other psychological disorders as well. For example, biofeedback data could enhance virtual environments for refusal skills training in substance abuse by ensuring that the stimuli provoke sufficient cravings. Conversely, skills training for autism spectrum disorder and psychotic disorders could be enhanced by using biofeedback data to modulate the virtual environment to decrease physiological arousal, increasing the likelihood that patients are not so overstimulated or stressed that learning new skills would be impossible.

Jin and colleagues (2016) used biofeedback in a VR intervention designed to reduce chronic pain. In this immersive intervention, patients used a treadmill to navigate through a virtual forest while implementing mindfulness and relaxation strategies. As patients' skin conductance lowered, the fog within the forest gradually dissolved, revealing visually engaging and picturesque forest views. This intervention incorporated biofeedback to provide positive reinforcement of patients' successful use of chronic pain management skills in an engaging and motivating manner.

Conclusion

There is considerable evidence demonstrating the utility of implementing VR into psychotherapy. While the currently available technology can enhance treatment outcomes, the full potential of VR psychotherapy remains untapped. Advancements in AI-based, dynamic environments that respond to patient behaviours, gestures and physiological reactions could revolutionise the treatment of many mental health conditions. Notwithstanding the potential benefits, one of the factors limiting the adoption of VR technology into clinical practice is the dearth of psychotherapy-specific software developed by clinicians who understand the complexities of psychological interventions and patients' needs. There are isolated research groups and clinical entrepreneurs developing this software, but they often work in isolation, without consulting or collaborating with other researchers or institutions to develop readily available VR intervention tools. Increasing and promoting collaboration would greatly enhance developments in this area.

12

Roadmap for Clinical Practice

Introduction

The previous sections of this book have described the research demonstrating that VR is a valuable tool to enhance psychotherapy. There is much evidence that virtual interventions can be as effective or more effective for a wide range of mental health disorders. Virtual technology holds tremendous potential for optimising patient outcomes while also increasing the cost-effectiveness of many types of psychotherapy. Moreover, when given the option, many patients choose virtual interventions over more traditional psychotherapy, which could further increase effectiveness by boosting patient engagement and motivation.

Despite solid empirical support, few mental health practitioners have incorporated virtual technology into their clinical practice. As there is currently no standardised training available for mental health practitioners, many are hesitant to embrace this technology, despite its potential for enhancing outcomes. The lack of clear guidelines for safe and ethical use of VR also underlies many clinicians' hesitancy about VR. Additionally, many practitioners find the process of comparing and selecting VR systems and accessories daunting.

This book was written to address some of these concerns and to help mental health practitioners learn more about VR technology, understand how to implement VR into clinical practice and consider which factors influence which patients could benefit most from this valuable therapeutic tool. The final section will present a roadmap for incorporating VR technology into clinical practice, from embracing AR/MR technology to psychotherapy in a fully realised metaverse (see Table 12.1).

DOI: 10.1201/b23370-15

TABLE 12.1

Roadmap summary: Phases, technologies, clinical applications and prerequisites

Phase	Technology	Clinical Application	Hardware Required	Key Prerequisites
Phase 1: AR/MR	Augmented reality via smartphone or tablet	Phobia exposure (e.g., spider/cockroach projection); initial XR-experience	Smartphone or tablet	Basic familiarity with AR apps; willingness to experiment
Phase 2: Partial VR	Commercial VR headsets with psychotherapy software packages	VR exposure therapy; relaxation training; behavioural activation as adjuncts to traditional therapy	VR headset (e.g., Meta Quest); psychotherapy software subscription	Clinician VR training; informed consent protocols; compatible hardware/software
Phase 3: VR Therapy	AI-driven, dynamic and customisable VR environments with biofeedback	All therapy components (assessments, psychoeducation, intervention, homework) are conducted in VR	Advanced headset with biofeedback sensors; high-speed internet	AI-based cue generation; fully customisable environments; standardised VR therapy training
Phase 4: Metaverse	Persistent virtual clinics within a fully realised metaverse	Global access to individual, group and support-group therapy; avatar-based interactions; AI-generated assessments	VR headset; metaverse platform access	Fully developed metaverse; ethical/regulatory frameworks; VR-specific billing codes

Phase 1: Embracing AR/MR

Augmented reality (AR) and mixed reality (MR) technology may be a cost-effective first step to incorporating extended reality (XR) technology into clinical practice. While research investigating the utility of AR and MR for psychotherapy is limited, these technologies have the potential to enhance therapeutic outcomes. For clinicians who would like experience with XR without investing in expensive VR goggles or headsets, AR is a viable first step.

For example, AR has demonstrated efficacy in treating phobias (Botella et al., 2005). Botella and colleagues used AR to superimpose images of cockroaches onto real-world images to treat a patient's cockroach phobia. In this study, AR was useful for projecting realistic images of cockroaches into the patient's environment and onto his person, so it appeared as though cockroaches were crawling on his hand. Following treatment with this AR-based exposure therapy, the patient reported significant decreases in fear and avoidance and could even approach, interact with and kill live cockroaches.

Similarly, Juan and colleagues (2005) used AR to treat a specific phobia in nine patients: five with cockroach phobias and four with spider phobias. AR was used to project images of the feared insects into the patients' environments and under boxes that patients were asked to lift. Following the AR intervention, all patients experienced a reduction in fear and avoidance and were able to approach, interact with and kill live cockroaches and spiders. Botella and colleagues (2010) replicated their original AR protocol for cockroach phobias and demonstrated that treatment gains were maintained over 3-, 6- and 12-month follow-ups.

The studies described above demonstrate the value of AR for psychotherapy by showing that AR evokes sufficient anxiety and distress for effective exposure therapy and that the habituation and new learning that occur during exposure sessions are durable and generalise to real-world behaviour. Baus and Bouchard (2014) highlight the differences between AR and VR that may make AR particularly useful for treating some phobias, OCD and other disorders. Unlike in VR, AR technology introduces virtual elements into the patients' natural physical environments. Moreover, during AR interventions, patients can see their own bodies (rather than a virtual body) interacting with the feared objects. These differences may strengthen new learning and facilitate generalisation more effectively and efficiently than *in vivo* exposure or VR-based exposure (Ventura et al., 2018).

AR has the potential to be a less expensive, but equally effective, alternative to immersive VR for addressing some mental health concerns, particularly for distressing stimuli for which real-world exposures are difficult or unethical. As a high percentage of the population possesses smartphones or tablets, this technology is highly accessible, especially because it is easier to set up and implement than VR systems. As such, adding AR/MR technology into clinical practice is a feasible first step for clinicians interested in therapy in the metaverse.

Phase 2: Partial Incorporation of VR

Most mental health practitioners treat a variety of mental health conditions. For these clinicians, fully incorporating VR into clinical practice may not be realistic, at least initially. While some VR software packages are designed to treat a range of disorders, it is unlikely that any one software package will be applicable or helpful for each patient treated by a practitioner. As such, clinicians must choose the software package that best meets the needs of their specific patient population.

There are a number of psychotherapy-specific software packages, including Virtually Better (https://virtuallybetter.com/products-overview/), PsyTech VR (www.psytechvr.com/), C2Care (www.c2.care/en/), XRHealth (https://ameliavirtualcare.com/), AppliedVR (www.appliedvr.io/) and Thera VR Inc. (www.theravr.io/), that offer a range of VR-based interventions for anxiety disorders, PTSD, addiction, pain management, depression, OCD and relaxation training. Some platforms include interventions from different theoretical orientations, like CBT, eye-movement desensitisation and reprocessing therapy (EMDR), dialectical behaviour therapy (DBT), acceptance and commitment therapy (ACT) and mindfulness-based stress reduction (MBSR).

These software platforms reflect remarkable innovations in VR technology for psychotherapists. However, as outlined earlier, the technology necessary for creating dynamic, adaptive and fully customisable virtual environments is not yet available. This means that, while these software platforms may be helpful for many patients, they do not allow clinicians to customise virtual environments to meet specific patient needs. This may be fine for clinicians treating anxiety disorders, combat-related PTSD or addiction, but VR-based interventions to address disorders that are more complex and idiosyncratic, like OCD, psychotic disorders and eating disorders will require more advanced technology.

Phase 3: Complete VR Therapy

Fully incorporating VR into psychotherapy is likely to depend on advances in AI-based cue generation that allow clinicians to customise dynamic virtual environments to meet the needs of each of their patients. Given the recent rapid developments in VR technology and AI, it is not unreasonable to believe that we could witness these developments within the next decade.

Full incorporation of VR into clinical practice would involve using VR technology for every step of the therapeutic process, including assessments, psychoeducation, interventions and homework. Again, it is worth mentioning that these advances would not remove the therapist from the process. The therapeutic relationship remains just as important, if not more important, in VR-based therapy as it does in more traditional forms of therapy. However, AI could decrease the therapist's workload by aggregating data from virtual assessments and intake forms and using this data to customise virtual interventions and homework assignments.

Moreover, several VR psychotherapy software packages include capabilities for remote VR-based psychotherapy, in both group and individual therapy formats. This increases access to evidence-based mental health treatments for patients whose geographic location, time/financial resources, symptoms or disabilities make in-person therapy inaccessible.

Phase 4: Psychotherapy in the Metaverse

Imagine a fully developed metaverse populated with virtual mental health clinics offering a broad range of mental health services. Patients and therapists located all over the globe could join together in private individual or group therapy sessions. Support groups, psychoeducation classes and skills training could be easily accessible to anyone in need. Patients could earn rewards for attendance, participation and completing therapy tasks (Usmani et al., 2022). The metaverse could drive new approaches to psychotherapy, like AVATAR therapy for psychosis and the full body illusion therapy for eating disorders. Additionally, the metaverse could include standardised, AI-generated functional assessments and behavioural tasks (Benrimoh et al., 2022).

According to the World Health Organization, mental illnesses are the leading cause of disability worldwide, yet as many as 70% of people who suffer from mental illness do not seek treatment (Henderson et al., 2013). In addition to removing geographical and other accessibility barriers, the metaverse would allow patients who prefer to remain anonymous due to the stigma of mental health challenges to fully participate in evidence-based practice by providing a more private virtual space to meet with practitioners (Yang, 2023). The case example below speculates how the metaverse could improve access to and the experience of psychotherapy for patients.

Case Example: Quinn

Quinn is a 34-year-old woman who has been suffering from germ-related OCD for over a decade. Her OCD symptoms have steadily worsened over the past three years, making it difficult for her to care for her three young children. She is a single mother who works full-time. Her symptoms often make her late for work, and she must return home to use the restroom. Her boss's patience is wearing thin, and she has been informed that she will be fired if this behaviour continues.

Until now, Quinn has been unable to attend therapy because she lives in a small rural town devoid of any mental health practitioners. She does not have the time or resources to drive to the nearest city, which is over an hour away, for therapy. Additionally, her OCD symptoms would make attending therapy in-person nearly impossible, as she is currently unable to use public restrooms.

A family member recently sent Quinn information on a virtual mental health clinic accessible in the metaverse and bought a VR system for her to use. As she completes the online registration for the virtual clinic, she is anxious, but hopeful. She is tired of living like this and knows that something has to change.

Part of the registration process involves creating an avatar to use in therapy. Quinn marvelled at how easy it had been to design an avatar that matched her personal style. It was so much easier than picking out an outfit, fixing her hair and makeup, all the while experiencing distressing obsessive thoughts about how she would manage the germs that she might encounter traveling to a therapist's office.

The day of Quinn's first session in the metaverse virtual clinic has arrived. She puts on her VR headset and enters the mental health clinic. She is relieved to see that it looks just as she imagined it. She is given a unique code to access her private virtual therapy room. As soon as she finishes entering the code, her surroundings shift, and she finds herself standing alongside a trickling mountain stream. The sounds of moving water, chirping birds and a low hum of insects fill her ears. Moving her head, she takes in the Rocky Mountains, snow still evident on the highest peaks. Quinn remembers that part of the new patient registration asked her to describe, in detail, the most peaceful place she had visited. She realises that her answer to this question has been used to create a therapy room specifically designed to put her at ease.

After a moment of appreciating the view, Quinn's therapist enters the virtual therapy environment. She takes in his dark hair and glasses, noting that his avatar looks exactly as she had expected from a therapist. As he introduces himself, he smiles, and his warm features convey a sense of invitation and openness. He instructs Quinn to walk along the river for several paces until they encounter two Adirondack chairs set up at an angle so that they can face each other, while still being able to look out over the river and the majestic mountain range. As they sit and begin to talk, Quinn's therapy journey in the metaverse begins.

Over the next several months, Quinn meets with her therapist weekly in the virtual mental health clinic. During the first sessions, he focuses on understanding how her OCD impacts her life and teaching Quinn about her obsessions and compulsions. Quinn engages in interactive exercises that demonstrate how she gets sucked into the OCD cycle of escalating obsessions, compulsions and avoidance. Quinn learns how her thoughts, feelings and behaviours reinforce each other and increase her distress once the cycle begins. She and her therapist collaborate to build a 3D exposure hierarchy to address her specific OCD triggers.

As she begins virtual exposure therapy, the peaceful mountain environment gives way to exposure environments based on her hierarchy.

In the first week, Quinn challenges herself to stand inside a clean public restroom for ten minutes without performing any rituals. She is surprised by how, even though she knows she is not really in a public bathroom, her body and brain do not seem to understand this. As soon as she walks into the virtual bathroom, her heart starts pounding, and she can feel the pressure of her blood pulsing in her veins. She tells her therapist that she can hear her heartbeat pounding in her ears. Her stomach drops, like she is on a rollercoaster, and beads of sweat gather on her forehead and upper lip.

Her therapist uses biofeedback sensors inside her VR headset to monitor her anxiety during these exposures. After Quinn completes each exposure, he shows her a 3D graph of her heart rate, blood pressure and respiration. She marvels at the spike in all three at the beginning of each exposure and then notices the long plateau that shows how she forced herself to stay in the bathroom, and then finally the downward slope as her body begins to relax. Habituation, her therapist calls it. Quinn had not believed him when he told her that it would happen, but there it is, in a graph, plain as day.

As the weeks pass, Quinn works her way through her hierarchy and ultimately confronts her greatest OCD trigger. She feels almost euphoric, realising that she not only managed to stand inside a filthy public bathroom, with walls covered in faeces and vomit, but that she had been able to touch those walls and then her own face and hair. As she looks at the biofeedback graphs after the exposure, she is stunned to see that, while there are still spikes in heart rate, blood pressure and respiration, those spikes are not nearly as high as those from earlier exposures. It is like watching in real-time as her brain begins to understand that there really is no danger.

One of Quinn's favourite parts about therapy in the metaverse is that she gets to attend weekly virtual support groups. Other people from all over the country and some from other countries gather to talk about OCD and therapy. It is such a relief to be around people who understand what she is going through. Many of the group members have found that it is not only the virtual exposures that are becoming easier and easier, but things in the real world no longer evoke the same level of distress. Most people find that their obsessive thoughts bother them less now that they understand that they are just thoughts, just false alarms, really. Now that they have experienced first-hand how their brains and bodies can react to virtual things as though they are real, it is much easier to discount distressing thoughts or impulses as simple by-products of a malfunctioning system. Like other group members, Quinn feels empowered by her success in therapy and begins reclaiming her life.

Quinn says that she feels safe in the metaverse. She can share her most bizarre obsessions and compulsions without fear of being laughed at or mocked. She feels free to express herself fully and is surprised by how many people feel the same way she does. She had not realised how much she had missed connecting with other people and how isolated her OCD had made her. Now she starts reaching out to people in real life, too. Yesterday she had lunch with the mom of one of the girls in her daughter's karate class. Three months ago, that would have been impossible.

Quinn appreciates the holistic approach of the virtual mental health clinic, where traditional therapies like cognitive behavioural therapy are combined with virtual exposure therapy and mindfulness meditation. She discovers that the more she practises mindfulness in the virtual environment, the easier it is to use those skills when she feels stressed or anxious in the real world. Not only have her OCD symptoms faded into little more than background noise, but she also feels more connected and fulfilled than she has in years. She has made friends with several people from the virtual support groups and is meeting new people in real life, too. Now that she is free from the time-consuming obsessions and compulsions, she has time to exercise, read and plant the garden she has always wanted.

Conclusion

Rapid advances in hardware and software over the past decade have catapulted VR into new domains, like healthcare and education. In addition to becoming more affordable and portable, the audio and visual capabilities of VR headsets have enabled the creation of increasingly realistic virtual environments. Improvements in hand tracking, haptic feedback and biofeedback devices have increased the utility of VR for psychotherapeutic interventions. While several companies now offer psychotherapy-specific VR software, full incorporation of VR into clinical practice depends on the ability to generate customisable and dynamic virtual environments to meet specific patient needs.

While the metaverse is not yet fully realised, it is coming. The possibilities for improvements in mental healthcare via the metaverse are exciting and seem nearly limitless. However, as with any new technology, mental healthcare within the metaverse is not without risks. Clinicians and other mental health professionals must be well-versed in the ethical considerations posed by this new technology and must keep their patients' safety and privacy at the forefront. By presenting both the exciting possibilities and the potential risks, this book is an attempt to initiate discussion of how best to use this technology to enhance psychotherapy while protecting patients.

References

Aafjes-van Doorn, K., Békés, V., & Prout, T. A. (2021). Grappling with our therapeutic relationship and professional self-doubt during COVID-19: will we use video therapy again? *Counseling Psychology Quarterly*, 34(3–4), 473–484. https://doi.org/10.1080/09515070.2020.1773404

Abramowitz, J. S. (2006). The psychological treatment of obsessive-compulsive disorder. *Canadian Journal of Psychiatry*, 51(7), 407–416. https://doi.org/10.1177/070674370605100702

Abramowitz, J. S., Taylor, S., & McKay, D. (2009). Obsessive-compulsive disorder. *The Lancet*, 374, 491–499. http://dx.doi.org/10.1016/S0140-6736(09)60240-3

Adery, L. H., Ichinose, M., Torregrossa, L. J., Wade, J., Nichols, H., Bekele, E., Bian, D., Gizdic, A., Granholm, E., Sarkar, J., & Park, S. (2018). The acceptability and feasibility of a novel virtual reality based social skills training game for schizophrenia: preliminary findings. *Psychiatry Research*, 270, 496–502. https://doi.org/10.1016/j.psychres.2018.10.014

Ahmad, M., Mohammad, E. B., & Anshasi, H. A. (2020). Virtual reality technology for pain and anxiety management among patients with cancer: a systematic review. *Pain Management Nursing*, 21(6), 601–607. https://doi.org/10.1016/j.pmn.2020.04.002

American Psychiatric Association. (2013). *Diagnostic and statistical manual of mental disorders* (5th ed.). https://doi.org/10.1176/appi.books.9780890425596

Anderson, P. L., Edwards, S. M., & Goodnight, J. R. (2017). Virtual reality and exposure group therapy for social anxiety disorder: results from a 4–6 year follow-up. *Cognitive Therapy Research*, 41, 230–236. https://doi.org/10.1007/s10608-016-9820-y

Anderson, P. L., Zimand, E., Hodges, L. F., & Rothbaum, B. O. (2005). Cognitive behavioral therapy for public-speaking anxiety using virtual reality for exposure. *Depression & Anxiety*, 22, 156–158. https://doi.org/10.1002/da.20090

Andronico, M. (2024, July 10). Meta Quest 2 review – a solid entry-level VR headset. *Tom's Guide*. www.tomsguide.com/reviews/oculus-quest-2-review

Bajaj, B., Robins, R., & Pande, N. (2016). Mediating role of self-esteem on the relationship between mindfulness, anxiety, and depression. *Personality and Individual Differences*, 96, 127–131. https://doi.org/10.1016/j.paid.2016.02.085

Baños, R. M, Etchemendy, E., Farfallini, L., Garcia-Palacios, A., Quero, S., & Botella, C. (2014). EARTH of well-being system: a pilot study of an information and communication technology-based positive psychology intervention. *The Journal of Positive Psychology*, 9, 482–488. https://doi.org/10.1080/17439760.2014.927906

Baus, O., & Bouchard, S. (2014). Moving from virtual reality exposure-based therapy to augmented reality exposure-based therapy: a review. *Frontiers in Human Neuroscience*, 8, 112. https://doi.org/10.3389/fnhum.2014.00112

Bekele, E., Crittendon, J., Zheng, Z., Swanson, A., Weitlauf, A., Warren, Z., & Sarkar, N. (2014). Assessing the utility of a virtual environment for enhancing facial affect recognition in adolescents with autism. *Journal of Autism and Developmental Disorders*, 44(7), 1641–1650. https://doi.org/10.1007/s10803-014-2035-8

Bell, I. H., Nicholas, J., Alvarez-Jimenez, M., Thompson, A., & Valmaggia, L. (2020). Virtual reality as a clinical tool in mental health research and practice. *Dialogues in Clinical Neuroscience*, 22(2), 169–177. https://doi.org/10.31887/DCNS.2020.22.2/lvalmaggia

Bellanti, D. M., Kelber, M. S., Workman, D. E., Beech, E. H., & Belsher, B. E. (2022). Rapid review on the effectiveness of telehealth interventions for the treatment of behavioral health disorders. *Military Medicine*, 187(5–6), e577–e588. https://doi.org/10.1093/milmed/usab318

Benbow, A. A., & Anderson, P. L. (2019). A meta-analytic examination of attrition in virtual reality exposure therapy for anxiety disorders. *Journal of Anxiety Disorders*, 61, 18–26. https://doi.org/10.1016/j.janxdis.2018.06.006

Benrimoh, D., Chheda, F. D., & Margolese, H. C. (2022). The best predictor of the future—the metaverse, mental health, and lessons learned from current technologies. *JMIR Mental Health*, 9(10), e40410. https://doi.org/10.2196/40410

Berkhof, M., van der Stouwe, E. C. D., Lestestuiver, B., van't Hag, E., van Grunsven, R., de Jager, J., Kooijmans, E., Zandee, C. E. R., Staring A.B.P., Pot-Kolder, R. M. C. A., Vos, M., & Veling, W. (2021). Virtual reality cognitive-behavioral therapy versus cognitive behavioral therapy for paranoid delusions: a study protocol for a single-blind multi-Centre randomized controlled superiority trial. *BMC Psychiatry*, 21, 496. https://doi.org/10.1186/s12888-021-03473-y

Botella, C. M., Juan, M. C., Baños, R. M., Alcañiz, M., Guillén, V., & Rey, B. (2005). Mixing realities? An application of augmented reality for the treatment of cockroach phobia. *Cyberpsychology & Behavior*, 8(2), 162–171. https://doi.org/10.1089/cpb.2005.8.162

Botella, C., Bretón-López, J., Quero, S., Baños, R. M., & García-Palacios, A. (2010). Treating cockroach phobia with augmented reality. *Behavior Therapy*, 41, 401–413. https://doi.org/10.1016/j.beth.2009.07.002

Bryant, F. B. (2003). Savoring beliefs inventory (SBI): a scale for measuring beliefs about savoring. *Journal of Mental Health*, 12(2), 175–196. https://doi.org/10.1080/0963823031000103489

Burden, D., & Savin-Baden, M. (2025). *The metaverse: A critical introduction*. Chapman & Hall.

Butler, A. C., Chapman, J. E., Forman, E. M., & Beck, A. T. (2006). The empirical status of cognitive-behavioral therapy: a review of meta-analyses. *Clinical Psychology Review*, 26(1), 17–31. https://doi.org/10.1016/j.cpr.2005.07.003

Butler, D., & Moseley, G. L. (2013). *Explain pain* (2nd ed.). NOIgroup Publications.

Carl, E., Stein, A. T., Levihn-Coon, A., Pogue, J. R., Rothbaum, B., Emmelkamp, P., Asmundson, G. J. G., Carlbring, P., & Powers, M. B. (2019). Virtual reality exposure therapy for anxiety and related disorders: a meta-analysis of randomized controlled trials. *Journal of Anxiety Disorders*, 61, 27–36. https://doi.org/10.1016/j.janxdis.2018.08.003

Carlbring, P., Westling, B. E., Ljungstrand, P., Ekselius, L., & Andersson, G. (2001). Treatment of panic disorder via the Internet: a randomized trial of a self-help program. *Behavior Therapy*, 32, 751–764. https://doi.org/10.1016/S0005-7894(01)80019-8

Carson, S. H., & Langer, E. J. (2006). Mindfulness and self-acceptance. *Journal of Rational-Emotive & Cognitive-Behavior Therapy*, 24(1), 29–43. https://doi.org/10.1007/s10942-006-0022-5

Carter, J. C., Blackmore, E., Sutandar-Pinnock, K., & Woodside, D. B. (2004). Relapse in anorexia nervosa: a survivor analysis. *Psychological Medicine*, 34(4), 671–679. https://doi.org/10.1017/S0033291703001168

Carter, R. (2024, January 12). The best VR gloves in 2024: harnessing haptic feedback. *XR Today*. www.xrtoday.com/virtual-reality/the-best-vr-gloves-in-2024-harnessing-haptic-feedback/

Caver, K. A., Shearer, E. M., Burks, D. J., Perry, K., De Paul, N. F., McGinn, M. M., & Felker, B. L. (2020). Telemental health training in the Veterans Administration Puget Sound health care system. *Journal of Clinical Psychology*, 76, 1108–1124. https://doi.org/10.1002/jclp.22797

Cesa, G. L., Manzoni, G. M., Bacchetta, M., Castelnuovo, G., Conti, S., Gaggioli, A., Mantovani, G., Molinari, E., Cardenas-Lopez, G., & Riva, G. (2013). Virtual reality for enhancing the cognitive behavioral treatment of obesity with binge eating disorder: randomized controlled study with one-year follow-up. *Journal of Medical Internet Research*, 15(6), e113. https://doi.org/10.2196/jmir.2441

Chen, K., Barnes-Horowitz, N., Treanor, M., Sun, M., Young, K. S., & Craske, M. G. (2021). Virtual reality reward training for anhedonia: a pilot study. *Frontiers in Psychology*, 11, 613617. https://doi.org/10.3389/fpsyg.2020.613617

Chen, Y. F., Huang, X. Y., Chien, C. H., & Cheng, J. F. (2017). The effectiveness of diaphragmatic breathing relaxation training for reducing anxiety. *Perspectives in Psychiatric Care*, 53, 329–336. https://doi.org/10.1111/ppc.12184

Cheng, Y., Huang, C.-L., & Yang, C.-S. (2015). Using a 3D immersive virtual environment system to enhance social understanding and social skills for children with autism spectrum disorders. *Focus on Autism and Other Developmental Disabilities*, 30(4), 222–236. https://doi.org/10.1177/1088357615583473

Cherestal, S., Schare, M. L., Grimaldi, S., Costello, K., & DeJesus, C. (2021). Remotely conducted versus office-based virtual reality treatment for aviophobia: questions of feasibility and accessibility. *Translational Issues in Psychological Science*, 7(3), 218–228. https://doi.org/10.1037/tps0000303

Chirico, A., Lucidi, F., De Laurentiis, M., Milanese, C., Napoli, A., & Giordano, A. (2016). Virtual reality in health system: beyond entertainment. A mini-review on the efficacy of VR during cancer treatment. *Journal of Cellular Physiology*, 231(2), 275–287. https://doi.org/10.1002/jcp.25117

Colombo, D., Suso-Ribera, C., Ortigosa-Beltran, I., Fernandez-Alvarez, J., Garcia-Palacios, A., & Botella, C. (2022). Behavioral activation through virtual reality for depression: a single-case experimental design with multiple baselines. *Journal of Clinical Medicine*, 11, 1262. https://doi.org/10.3390/jcm11051262

Conrad, A., & Roth, W. T. (2007). Muscle relaxation therapy for anxiety disorders: it works but how? *Journal of Anxiety Disorders*, 21(3), 243–264. https://doi.org/10.1016/j.janxdis.2006.08.001

Cote, S., & Bouchard, S. (2009). Cognitive mechanisms underlying virtual reality exposure. *CyberPsychology & Behavior*, 12(2), 121–129. https://doi.org/10.1089/cpb.2008.0008

Craig, A., Brown, E., Upright, J., & DeRosier, M. (2016). Enhancing children's social-emotional functioning through virtual game-based delivery of social skills training. *Journal of Child & Family Studies*, 25(3), 959–968. https://doi.org/10.1007/s10826-015-0274-8

Craig, T., Rus-Calafell, M. D. M. R., Ward, T., Leff, J. P., Huckvale, M., Howarth, E., Emsley, R. A., & Garety, P. (2018). AVATAR therapy for auditory verbal hallucinations in people with psychosis: a single-blind, randomized controlled trial. *Lancet Psychiatry*, 5, 31–40. https://doi.org/10.1016/S2215-0366(17)30427-3

Craske, M. G., Kircanski, K., Zelikowsky, M., Mystkowski, J., Chowdhury, N., & Baker, A. (2008). Optimizing inhibitory learning during exposure therapy. *Behavior Research and Therapy*, 46, 5–27. https://doi.org/10.1016/j.brat.2007.10.003

Crockett, S. (2023, October 22). AI-Driven virtual reality: creating dynamic and interactive virtual environments. *Medium*. https://medium.com/@shomariccrockett/ai-driven-virtual-reality-creating-dynamic-and-interactive-virtual-environments-6137fbfd2d2d

Cross, A. (2023, November 9). The evolution of virtual reality: exploring the past, present, and future. *Forbes*. www.forbes.com/sites/forbesbusinesscouncil/2023/11/09/the-evolution-of-virtual-reality-exploring-the-past-present-and-future/?sh=3d4f30f2b70f

Dakanalis, A., Gaudio, S., Serino, S., Clerici, M., Carra, G., & Riva, G. (2016). Body-image distortion in anorexia nervosa. *Nature Reviews Disease Primers*, 2, 16026. https://doi.org/10.1038/nrdp.2016.26

Darnall, B. D., Krishnamurthy, P., Tsuei, J., & Minor, J. D. (2020). Self-administered skills-based virtual reality intervention for chronic pain: randomized controlled pilot study. *JMIR Formative Research*, 4(7), e17293. https://doi.org/10.2196/17293

Davis, K. A., Zhao, F., Janis, R. A., Castonguay, L. G., Hayes, J. A., & Scofield, B. E. (2023). Therapeutic alliance and clinical outcomes in teletherapy and in-person psychotherapy: a non-inferiority study during the COVID-19 pandemic. *Psychotherapy Research*, 1–12. https://doi.org/10.1080/10503307.2023.2229505

Deacon, B. J., & Abramowitz, J. S. (2004). Cognitive and behavioral treatments for anxiety disorders: a review of meta-analytic findings. *Journal of Clinical Psychology*, 60(4), 429–441. https://doi.org/10.1002/jclp.10255

Dellazizzo, L., Potvin, S., Phraxayavong, K., & Dumais, A. (2021). One-year randomized trial comparing virtual reality-assisted therapy to cognitive-behavioral therapy for patients with treatment-resistant schizophrenia. *Schizophrenia*, 7, 9. https://doi.org/10.1038/s41537-021-00139-2

Didehbani, N., Allen, T., Kandalaft, M., Krawczyk, D., & Chapman, S. (2016). Virtual reality social cognition training for children with high functioning autism. *Computers in Human Behavior*, 62, 703–711. https://doi.org/10.1016/j.chb.2016.04.033

Difede, J., Cukor, J., Jayasinghe, N., Patt, I., Jedel, S., Spielman, L., Giosan, C., & Hoffman, H. G. (2007). Virtual reality exposure therapy for the treatment of posttraumatic stress disorder following September 11, 2001. *Journal of Clinical Psychiatry*, 68(11), 1639–1647. https://doi.org/10.4088/jcp.v68n1102

Du Sert, O. P., Potvin, S., Lipp, O., Dellazizzo, L., Laurelli, M., Breton, R., LaLonde, P., Phraxayavong, K., O'Connor, K., Pelletier, J. -F., Boukhalfi, T., Renaud, P., & Dumais, A. (2018). Virtual reality therapy for refractory auditory verbal hallucinations in schizophrenia: a pilot clinical trial. *Schizophrenia Research*, 197, 176–181. https://doi.org/10.1016/j.schres.2018.02.031

Dua, D., Jagota, G., & Grover, S. (2021). Management of obsessive-compulsive disorder with virtual reality-based exposure. *Industrial Psychiatry Journal*, 30, 179–181. https://doi.org/10.4103/ipj.ipj_33_19

Eddy, K. T., Dutra, L., Bradley, R., & Westen, D. (2004). A multidimensional meta-analysis of psychotherapy and pharmacotherapy for obsessive-compulsive disorder. *Clinical Psychology Review*, 24(8), 1011–1030. https://doi.org/10.1016/j.cpr.2004.08.004

Ehde, D. M., Dillworth, T. M., & Turner, J. A. (2014). Cognitive-behavioral therapy for individuals with chronic pain: efficacy, innovations, and directions for research. *American Psychologist*, 69(2), 153–166. https://doi.org/10.1037/a0035747

Falkenström, F., Granström, F., & Holmqvist, R. (2013). Therapeutic alliance predicts symptomatic improvement session by session. *Journal of Counseling Psychology*, 60(3), 317–328. https://doi.org/10.1037/a0032258

Farrell, C., & Shafran, R. (2006). Empirically evaluated treatments for body image disturbance: a review. *European Eating Disorders Review*, 14, 289–300. https://doi.org/10.1002/erv.693

Ferrer-García, M., Gutiérrez-Maldonado, J., Pla-Sanjuanelo, J., Vilalta-Abella, F., Riva, G., Clerici, M., Ribas-Sabaté, J., Andreu-Garcia, A., Fernandez-Aranda, F., Forcano, L., Riesco, N., Sánchez, I., Escandón-Nagel, N., Gomez-Tricio, O., Tena, V., & Dakanalis, A. (2017). A randomized controlled comparison of second-level treatment approaches for treatment-resistant adults with bulimia nervosa and binge eating disorder: assessing the benefits of virtual reality cue exposure therapy. *European Eating Disorders Review*, 25, 479–490. https://doi.org/10.1002/erv.2538

Ferrer-García, M., Pla-Sanjuanelo, J., Dakanalis, A., Vilalta-Abella, F., Riva, G., Fernandez-Aranda, F., Forcano, L., Riesco, N., Sánchez, I., Clerici, M., Ribas-Sabaté, J., Andreu-Garcia, A., Escandón-Nagel, N., Gomez-Tricio, O., Tena, V., & Gutiérrez-Maldonado, J. (2019). A randomized trial of virtual reality-based cue exposure second-level therapy and cognitive behavior second-level therapy for bulimia nervosa and binge-eating disorder: outcome at six-month follow-up. *Cyberpsychology, Behavior, and Social Networking*, 22, 60–68. https://doi.org/10.1089/cyber.2017.0675

Flückiger, C., Del Re, A. C., Wampold, B. E., & Horvath, A. O. (2018). The alliance in adult psychotherapy: a meta-analytic synthesis. *Psychotherapy*, 55(4), 316–340. https://doi.org/10.1037/pst0000172

Foa, E. B., & Kozak, M. J. (1986). Emotional processing of fear: exposure to corrective information. *Psychological Bulletin*, 99(1), 20–35. https://doi.org/10.1037/0033-2909.99.1.20

Foa, E. B., Liebowitz, M. R., Kozak, M. J., Davies, S., Campeas, R., Franklin, M. E., Huppert, J. D., Kjernisted, K., Rowan, V., Schmidt, A. B., Simpson, H. B., & Tu, X. (2005). Randomized, placebo-controlled trial of exposure and ritual prevention, clomipramine, and their combination in the treatment of obsessive-compulsive disorder. *American Journal of Psychiatry*, 162(1), 151–161. https://doi.org/10.1176/appi.ajp.162.1.151

Foa, E. B., & McLean, C. P. (2016). The efficacy of exposure therapy for anxiety-related disorders and its underlying mechanisms: the case of OCD and PTSD. *Annual Review of Clinical Psychology*, 12, 1–28. https://doi.org/10.1146/annurev-clinpsy-021815-093533

Freeman, D., Bradley, J., Antley, A., Bourke, E., DeWeever, N., Evans, N., Cernis, E., Sheaves, B., Waite, F., Dunn, G., Slater, M., & Clark, D. M. (2016). Virtual reality in the treatment of persecutory delusions: randomized controlled experimental study testing how to reduce delusional conviction. *The British Journal of Psychiatry*, 209, 62–67. https://doi.org/10.1192/bjp.bp.115.176438

Freeman, D., & Garety, P. (2014). Advances in understanding and treating persecutory delusions: a review. *Social Psychiatry and Psychiatric Epidemiology*, 49(8), 1179–1189. https://doi.org/10.1007/s00127-014-0928-7

Freeman, D., Haselton, P., Freeman, J., Spanlang, B., Kishore, S., Albery, E., Denne, M., Brown, P., Slater, M., & Nickless, A. (2018). Automated psychological therapy using immersive virtual reality for treatment of fear of heights: a single-blind, parallel-group, randomized controlled trial. *The Lancet Psychiatry*, 5(8), 625–632. https://doi.org/10.1016/S2215-0366(18)30226-8

Garcia-Palacios, A., Botella, C., Hoffman, H., & Fabregat, S. (2007). Comparing acceptance and refusal rates of virtual reality exposure vs. in vivo exposure by patients with specific phobias. *CyberPsychology & Behavior*, 10, 722–724. https://doi.org/10.1089/cpb.2007.9962

Giese-Davis, J., Collie, K., Rancourt, K. M. S., Neri, E., Kraemer, H. C., & Spiegel, D. (2011). Decrease in depression symptoms is associated with longer survival in patients with metastatic breast cancer: a secondary analysis. *Journal of Clinical Oncology*, 29, 413–420. https://doi.org/10.1200/JCO.2010.28.4455

Giovanetti, A. K., Punt, S. E. W., Nelson, E.-L., & Ilardi, S. S. (2022). Teletherapy versus in-person psychotherapy for depression: a meta-analysis of randomized controlled trials. *Telemedicine and e-Health*, 28(8), 1077–1089. https://doi.org/10.1089/tmj.2021.0294

Glueckauf, R. L., Maheu, M. M., Drude, K. P., Wells, B. A., Wang, Y., Gustafson, D. J., & Nelson, E.-L. (2018). Survey of psychologists' telebehavioral health practices: technology use, ethical issues, and training needs. *Professional Psychology: Research and Practice*, 49(3), 205–219. https://doi.org/10.1037/pro0000188

Gnacek, M., Broulidakis, J., Mavridou, I., Fatoorechi, M., Seiss, E., Kostoulas, T., Balaguer-Ballester, E., Kiprijanovska, I., Rosten, C., & Nduka, C. (2022). EmteqPRO—Fully integrated biometric sensing array for non-invasive biomedical research in virtual reality. *Frontiers in Virtual Reality*, 3, 781218. https://doi.org/10.3389/frvir.2022.781218

Godleski, L., Darkins, A., & Peters, J. (2012). Outcomes of 98,609 U.S. Department of Veterans Affairs patients enrolled in telemental health services 2006–2010. *Psychiatric Services*, 63, 383–385. https://doi.org/10.1176/appi.ps.201100206

Gorini, A., Griez, E., Petrova, A., & Riva, G. (2010). Assessment of the emotional responses produced by exposure to real food, virtual food and photographs of food in patients affected by eating disorders. *Annals of General Psychiatry*, 9, 30. https://doi.org/10.1186/1744-859X-9-30

Gould, R. A., Mueser, K. T., Bolton, E., Mays, V., & Goff, D. (2001). Cognitive therapy for psychosis in schizophrenia: an effect size analysis. *Schizophrenia Research*, 48, 335–342. https://doi.org/10.1016/s0920-9964(00)00145-6

Greenwald, W. (2024, July 10). Best VR Headsets for 2024. *PC Mag*. www.pcmag.com/lists/best-vr-headsets

Guillen-Sanz, H., Checa, D., Miguel-Alonso, I., & Bustillo, A. (2024). A systematic review of wearable biosensor usage in immersive virtual reality experiences. *Virtual Reality*, 28, 74. https://doi.org/10.1007/s10055-024-00970-9

Hayes, S. (2022, November). Are counselors ready for the metaverse? *Counseling Today*. www.counseling.org/publications/counseling-today-magazine/article-archive/article/legacy/are-counselors-ready-for-the-metaverse

Henderson, C., Evans-Lacko, S., & Thornicroft, G. (2013). Mental illness stigma, help seeking, and public health programs. *American Journal of Public Health*, 103(5), 777–780. https://doi.org/10.2105/AJPH.2012.301056

Henderson, S., & Gilding, M. (2004). 'I've never clicked this much with anyone in my life': trust and hyperpersonal communication in online friendships. *New Media & Society*, 6(4), 487–506. https://doi.org/10.1177/146144804044331

Hernández-Serrano, O., Ghitâ, A., Figueras-Puigdeerrajols, N., Fernández-Ruiz, J., Monras, M., Ortega, L., Mondon, S., Teixidor, L., Gual, A., Ugas-Ballester, L., Fernández, M., Montserrat, R., Porras-Garcia, B., Ferrer-Garcia, M., & Gutiérrez-Maldonado, J. (2020). Predictors of changes in alcohol craving levels during a virtual reality cue exposure treatment among patients with alcohol use disorder. *Journal of Clinical Medicine*, 9, 3018. https://doi.org/10.3390/jcm9093018

Hoffman, B. M., Papas, R. K., Chatkoff, D. K., & Kerns, R. D. (2007). Meta-analysis of psychological interventions for chronic low back pain. *Health Psychology*, 26(1), 1–9. https://doi.org/10.1037/0278-6133.26.1.1

Holmberg, T. T., Eriksen, T. L., Petersen, R., Fredericksen, N. N., Damgaard-Sørensen, U., & Lichtenstein, M. B. (2020). Social anxiety can be triggered by 360-degree videos in virtual reality: a pilot study exploring fear of shopping. *Cyberpsychology, Behavior, and Social Networking*, 23(7), 495–499. https://doi.org/10.1089/cyber.2019.0295

Hopper, S. I., Murray, S. L., Ferrara, L. R., & Singleton, J. K. (2019). Effectiveness of diaphragmatic breathing on physiological and psychological stress in adults: a quantitative systematic review protocol. *JBI Database Systematic Reviews and Implementation Reports*, 9, 1855–1876. https://doi.org/10.11124/JBISRIR-2017-003848

Inozu, M., Celikcan, U., Akin, B., & Cicek, N. M. (2020). The use of virtual reality (VR) exposure for reducing contamination fear and disgust: can VR be an effective alternative exposure technique to in vivo? *Journal of Obsessive-Compulsive and Related Disorders*, 25, 100518. https://doi.org/10.1016/j.jocrd.2020.100518

Ionescu, A., Van Daele, T., Rizzo, A., Blair, C., & Best, P. (2021). 360° videos for immersive mental health interventions: a systematic review. *Journal of Technology in Behavioral Science*, 6, 631–651. https://doi.org/10.1007/s41347-021-00221-7

Jeong, H. S., Oh, J., Paik, M., Kim, H., Jang, S., Kim, B. S., & Kim, J.-J. (2022). Development and feasibility assessment of virtual reality-based relaxation self-training program. *Frontiers in Virtual Reality*, 2, 722558. https://doi.org/10.3389/frvir.2021.722558

Jin, W., Choo, A., Gromala, D., Shaw, C., & Squire, P. (2016). A virtual reality game for chronic pain management: a randomized, controlled clinical study. *Studies in Health Technology and Informatics*, 220, 154–160.

Jose, P. E., Lim, B. T., & Bryant, F. B. (2012). Does savoring increase happiness? A daily diary study. *The Journal of Positive Psychology*, 7(3), 176–187. https://doi.org/10.1080/17439760.2012.671345

Juan, M. C., Alcañiz, M., Botella, C. M., Baños, R. M., & Guerrero, B. (2005). Using augmented reality to treat phobias. *IEEE Computer Graphics and Applications*, 25, 31–37. https://doi.org/10.1109/MCG.2005.143

Kandalaft, M. R., Didehbani, N., Krawczyk, D. C., Allen, T. T., & Chapman, S. B. (2013). Virtual reality social cognition training for young adults with high-functioning autism. *Journal of Autism and Developmental Disorders*, 43, 34–44. https://doi.org/10.1007/s10803-012-1544-6

Ke, F., & Moon, J. (2018). Virtual collaborative gaming as social skills training for high-functioning autistic children. *British Journal of Educational Technology*, 49(4), 728–741. https://doi.org/10.1111/bjet.12626

Keizer, A., van Elburg, A., Helms, R., & Dijkerman, H. C. (2016). A virtual reality full body illusion improves body image disturbance in anorexia nervosa. *PLoS One*, 11(10), e0163921. https://doi.org/10.1371/journal.pone.0163921

Kim, H. E., Hong, Y.-J., Kim, M.-K., Jung, Y. H., Kyeong, S., & Kim, J.-J. (2017). Effectiveness of self-training using the mobile-based virtual reality program in patients with social anxiety disorder. *Computers in Human Behavior*, 73, 614–619. https://doi.org/10.1016/j.chb.2017.04.017

Kim, K., Kim, C.-H., Cha, K. R., Park, J., Han, K., Kim, Y. K., Kim, J., Kim, I. Y., & Kim, S. I. (2008). Anxiety provocation and measurement using virtual reality in patients with obsessive-compulsive disorder. *CyberPsychology and Behavior*, 11(6), 637–641. https://doi.org/10.1089/cpb.2008.0003

Krijn, M., Emmelkamp, P. M., Olafsson, R. P., & Biemond, R. (2004). Virtual reality exposure therapy of anxiety disorders: a review. *Clinical Psychology Review*, 24(3), 259–281. https://doi.org/10.1016/j.cpr.2004.04.001

Kritikos, J., Alevizopoulos, G., & Koutsouris, D. (2021). Personalized virtual reality human-computer interaction for psychiatric and neurological illnesses: a dynamically adaptive virtual reality environment that changes according to real-time feedback from electrophysiological signal responses. *Frontiers in Human Neuroscience*, 15, 596980. https://doi.org/10.3389/fnhum.2021.596980

Laforest, M., Bouchard, S., Bossé, J., & Mesly, O. (2016). Effectiveness of in virtuo exposure and response prevention treatment using cognitive-behavioral therapy for obsessive-compulsive disorder: a study based on a single-case study protocol. *Frontiers in Psychiatry*, 7, 99. https://doi.org/10.3389/fpsyt.2016.00099

Laforest, M., Bouchard, S., Cretu, A., & Mesly, O. (2016). Inducing an anxiety response using a contaminated virtual environment: validation of a therapeutic tool for obsessive-compulsive disorder. *Frontiers in ICT*, 3, 18. https://doi.org/10.3389/fict.2016.00018

Lamson, R., & Meisner, M. (1994). The effects of virtual reality immersion in the treatment of anxiety, panic and phobia of heights. In H. Murphy (Ed.), *Proceedings of the 2nd Annual Conference on Virtual Reality and Persons with Disabilities* (pp. 63–68). California State University, Northridge.

Landmark, J., Merskey, H., Cernovsky, Z., & Helms, E. (1990). The positive triad of schizophrenic symptoms. Its statistical properties and its relationship to 13 traditional diagnostic systems. *British Journal of Psychiatry*, 156, 388–394. https://doi.org/10.1192/bjp.156.3.388

Larson, E. B., Feigon, M., Gagliardo, P., & Dvorkin, A. Y. (2014). Virtual reality and cognitive rehabilitation: a review of current outcome research. *NeuroRehabilitation*, 34, 759–772. https://doi.org/10.3233/NRE-141078

Lee, K. (2023). Counseling psychological understanding and considerations of the metaverse: A theoretical review. *Healthcare*, 11(18), 2490. https://doi.org/10.3390/healthcare11182490

Leuchtenberg, S., Gromer, D., & Käthner, I. (2022). Videoconferencing versus face-to-face psychotherapy: insights from patients and psychotherapists about comparability of therapeutic alliance, empathy, and treatment characteristics. *Counseling & Psychotherapy Research*, 23(2), 389–403. https://doi.org/10.1002/capr.12538

Levy, F., Leboucher, P., Rautureau, G., & Jouvent, R. (2016). E-virtual reality exposure therapy in acrophobia: a pilot study. *Journal of Telemedicine and Telecare*, 22(4), 215–220. https://doi.org/10.1177/1357633X15598243

Li, M., Wang, L., Jiang, M., Wu, D., Tian, T., & Huang, W. (2020). Relaxation techniques for depressive disorders in adults: a systematic review and meta-analysis of randomized controlled trials. *International Journal of Psychiatry in Clinical Practice*, 24(3), 219–226. https://doi.org/10.1080/13651501.2020.1764587

Lin, T., Heckman, T. G., & Anderson, T. (2022). The efficacy of synchronous teletherapy versus in-person therapy: a meta-analysis of randomized clinical trials. *Clinical Psychology: Science and Practice*, 29(2), 167–178. https://doi.org/10.1037/cps0000056

Lindner, P., Miloff, A., Fagernas, S., Andersen, J., Sigeman, M., Andersson, G., Furmark, T., & Carlbring, P. (2019). Therapist-led and self-led one-session virtual reality exposure therapy for public speaking anxiety with consumer hardware and software: a randomized controlled trial. *Journal of Anxiety Disorders*, 61, 45–54. https://doi.org/10.1016/j.janxdis.2018.07.003

Lundin, J., Lundström, A., Gulliksen, J., Blendulf, J., Ejeby, K., Nyman, H., Björkander, D., & Hedman-Lagerlöf, E. (2021). Using 360-degree videos for virtual reality exposure in CBT for panic disorder with agoraphobia: a feasibility study. *Behavioural and Cognitive Psychotherapy*, 50(2), 158–170. https://doi.org/10.1017/S1352465821000473

Lundin, R. M., Yeap, Y., & Menkes, D. B. (2023). Adverse effects of virtual and augmented reality interventions in psychiatry: systematic review. *JMIR Mental Health*, 10, e43240. https://doi.org/10.2196/43240

Luo, H., Cao, C., Zhong, J., Chen, J., & Cen, Y. (2018). Adjunctive virtual reality for procedural pain management of burn patients during dressing change or physical therapy: a systematic review and meta-analysis of randomized controlled trials. *Wound Repair and Regeneration*, 27, 90–101. https://doi.org/10.1111/wrr.1

Ma, J., Zhao, D., Xu, N., & Yang, J. (2023). The effectiveness of immersive virtual reality (VR) based mindfulness training on improvement mental-health in adults: a narrative systematic review. *Explore*, 19(3), 310–318. https://doi.org/10.1016/j.explore.2022.08.001

Ma, L., Mor, S., Anderson, P. L., Baños, R. M., Botella, C., Bouchard, S., Cárdenas-López, G., Donker, T., Fernández-Álvarez, J., Lindner, P., Mühlberger, A., Powers, M. B., Quero, S., Rothbaum, B., Wiederhold, B. K., & Carlbring, P. (2021). Integrating virtual realities and psychotherapy: SWOT analysis on VR and MR based treatments of anxiety and stress-related disorders. *Cognitive Behaviour Therapy*, 50(6), 509–526. https://doi.org/10.1080/16506073.2021.1939410

Ma, X., Yue, Z. Q., Gong, Z. Q., Zhang, H., Duan, N. Y., Shi, Y. T., Wei, G. X., & Li, Y. F. (2017). The effect of diaphragmatic breathing on attention, negative affect and stress in healthy adults. *Frontiers in Psychology*, 8, 874. https://doi.org/10.3389/fpsyg.2017.00874

Marco, J. H., Perpiña, C., & Botella, C. (2013). Effectiveness of cognitive behavioral therapy supported by virtual reality in the treatment of body image in eating disorders: one-year follow-up. *Psychiatry Research*, 209(3), 619–625. https://doi.org/10.1016/j.psychres.2013.02.023

Matsangidou, M., Otkhmezuri, B., Ang, C. S., Avraamides, M., Riva, G., Gaggioli, A., Iosif, D., & Karekla, M. (2020). "Now I can see me" designing a multi-user virtual reality remote psychotherapy for body weight and shape concerns. *Human-Computer Interaction*, 37(4), 314–340. https://doi.org/10.1080/07370024.2020.1788945

Mayo-Wilson, E., Dias, S., Mavranezouli, J., Kew, K., Clark, D. M., Ades, A. E., & Pilling, S. (2014). Psychological and pharmacological interventions for social anxiety disorder in adults: a systematic review and network meta-analysis. *The Lancet Psychiatry*, 1(5), 368–376. https://doi.org/10.1016/S2215-0366(14)70329-3

Melzack, R., & Wall, P. D. (1965). Pain mechanisms: a new theory. *Science*, 150, 971–979. https://doi.org/10.1126/science.150.3699.971

Meyerbröker, K. (2014). Virtual reality exposure therapy. In P. Emmelkamp & T. Ehring (Eds.), *The Wiley handbook of anxiety disorders, Vol. 1. Theory and research; Vol. 2. Clinical assessment and treatment* (pp. 1310–1324). Wiley Blackwell.

Meyerbroker, K., & Emmelkamp, P. M. G. (2010). Virtual reality exposure therapy in anxiety disorders: a systematic review of process-and-outcome studies. *Depression and Anxiety*, 27, 933–944. https://doi.org/10.1002/da.20734

Meyerbroker, K., Morina, N., Kerkhof, G. A., & Emmelkamp, P. M. G. (2022). Potential predictors of virtual reality exposure therapy for fear of flying: anxiety sensitivity, self-efficacy and the therapeutic alliance. *Cognitive Therapy and Research*, 46, 646–654. https://doi.org/10.1007/s10608-021-10269-7

Mitsea, E., Drigas, A., & Skianis, C. (2023). Virtual reality mindfulness for meta-competence training among people with different mental disorders: a systematic review. *Psychiatry International*, 4(4), 324–353. https://doi.org/10.3390/psychiatryint4040031

Morina, N., Brinkman, W-P., Hartanto, D., Kampmann, I. L., & Emmelkamp, P. M. G. (2015). Social interactions in virtual reality exposure therapy: a proof-of-concept pilot study. *Technology and Health Care*, 23, 581–589. https://doi.org/10.3233/THC-151014

Nameth, K., Brown, R., Bullock, K., Adler, S., Riva, G., Safer, D., & Runfola, C. (2021). Translating virtual reality cue exposure therapy for binge eating into a real-world setting: an uncontrolled pilot study. *Journal of Clinical Medicine*, 10, 1511. https://doi.org/10.3390/jcm10071511

Nathan, P. E., & Gorman, J. M. (Eds.). (2002). *A guide to treatments that work*. Oxford University Press.

Nichols, S., & Patel, H. (2002). Health and safety implications of virtual reality: a review of empirical evidence. *Applied Ergonomics*, 33(3), 251–271. https://doi.org/10.1016/s0003-6870(02)00020-0

Norcross, J. C. (2001). Purposes, processes, and products of the task force on empirically supported therapy relationships. *Psychotherapy: Theory, Research, Practice, Training*, 38(4), 345–356. https://doi.org/10.1037/0033-3204.38.4.345

Norcross, J. C., Pfund, R. A., & Prochaska, J. O. (2013). Psychotherapy in 2022: a Delphi poll on its future. *Professional Psychology: Research and Practice*, 44(5), 363–370. https://doi.org/10.1037/a0034633

Opris, D., Pintea, S., García-Palacios, A., Botella, C., Szarmosközi, S., & David, D. (2012). Virtual reality exposure therapy in anxiety disorders: a quantitative meta-analysis. *Depression & Anxiety*, 29(2), 85–93. https://doi.org/10.1002/da.20910

Öst, L.-G., Havnen, A., Hansen, B., & Kvale, G. (2015). Cognitive-behavioral treatments of obsessive-compulsive disorder. A systematic review and meta-analysis of studies published 1993–2014. *Clinical Psychology Review*, 40, 156–169. https://doi.org/10.1016/j.cpr.2015.06.003

Oyama, H., Ohsuga, M., Tatsuno, Y., & Katsumata, N. (1999). Evaluation of the psychological effectiveness of the bedside wellness system. *CyberPsychology & Behavior*, 2, 81–84. https://doi.org/10.1089/cpb.1999.2.81

Palekar, T. J., Mokashi, M. G., Anwer, S., Kakrani, A. L., Khandare, S. D., & Alghadir, A. H. (2015). Effect of galvanic skin resistance-aided biofeedback training in reducing the pulse rate, respiratory rate, and blood pressure due to perceived stress in physiotherapy students. *Turkish Journal of Physical Medicine and Rehabilitation*, 61, 116–119. https://doi.org/10.5152/tftrd.2015.97957

Pardini, S., Gabrielli, S., Olivetto, S., Fusina, F., Dianti, M., Forti, S., Lancini, C., & Novara, C. (2024). Personalized virtual reality compared with guided imagery for enhancing the impact of progressive muscle relaxation training: pilot randomized controlled trial. *JMIR Mental Health*, 11, e48649. https://doi.org/10.2196/48649

Parsons, S., & Mitchell, P. (2002). The potential of virtual reality in social skills training for people with autistic spectrum disorders. *Journal of Intellectual Disability Research*, 46(5), 430–443.

Paul, M., Bullock, K., & Bailenson, J. (2020). Virtual reality behavioral activation as an intervention for major depressive disorder: case report. *JMIR Mental Health*, 7(11), e24331. https://doi.org/10.2196/24331

Perciavalle, V., Blandini, M., Fecarotta, P., Buscemi, A., Di Corrado, D., Bertolo, L., & Coco, M. (2017). The role of deep breathing on stress. *Neurological Sciences*, 38, 451–458. https://doi.org/10.1007/s10072-016-2790-8

Perpiñá, C., Baños, R.M., Botella, C., & Marco, J. H. (2001). Virtual reality as a therapy tool: a case study on body image alteration disorders. *Revista Argentina de Clinica Psicológia*, 10, 227–241.

Perpiñá, C., Roncero, M., Fernandez-Aranda, F., Jimenez-Murcia, S., Forcano, L., & Sanchez, I. (2013). Clinical validation of a virtual environment for normalizing eating patterns in eating disorders. *Comprehensive Psychiatry*, 54(6), 680–686. https://doi.org/10.1016/j.comppsych.2013.01.007

Pierce, B. S., Perrin, P. B., Tyler, C. M., McKee, G. B., & Watson, J. D. (2020). The COVID-19 telepsychology revolution: a national study of pandemic-based changes in U.S. mental health care delivery. *American Psychologist*, 76(1), 14–25. https://doi.org/10.1037/amp0000722

Porras-Garcia, B., Ferrer-Garcia, M., Serrano-Troncoso, E., Carulla-Roig, M., Soto-Usera, P., Miquel-Nabau, H., Fernández-Del Castillo Olivares, L., Marnet-Fiol, R., de la Montaña Santos-Carrasco, I., Borszewski, B., Díaz-Marsá, M., Sánchez-Díaz, I., Fernández-Aranda, F., & Gutiérrez-Maldonado, J. (2021). AN-VR-BE. A randomized controlled trial for reducing fear of gaining weight and other eating disorder symptoms in anorexia nervosa through virtual reality-based body exposure. *Journal of Clinical Medicine*, 10, 682. https://doi.org/10.3390/jcm10040682

Pourmand, A., Davis, S., Marchak, A., Whiteside, T., & Sikka, N. (2018). Virtual reality as a clinical tool for pain management. *Current Pain and Headache Reports*, 22, 1–6. https://doi.org/10.1007/s11916-018-0708-2

Powers, M. B., & Emmelkamp, P. M. G. (2008). Virtual reality exposure therapy for anxiety disorders: a meta-analysis. *Journal of Anxiety Disorders*, 22, 561–569. https://doi.org/10.1016/j.janxdis.2007.04.006

Price, M., & Anderson, P. (2007). The role of presence in virtual reality exposure therapy. *Journal of Anxiety Disorders*, 21(5), 742–751. https://doi.org/10.1016/j.janxdis.2006.11.002

Quero, S., Perez-Ara, M. A., Breton-Lopez, J., Garcia-Palacios, A., Baños, R.M., & Botella, C. (2014). Acceptability of virtual reality interoceptive exposure for the treatment of panic disorder with agoraphobia. *British Journal of Guidance and Counselling*, 42(2), 123–137. https://doi.org/10.1080/03069885.2013.852159

Ready, D. J., Pollack, S., Rothbaum, B. O., & Alarcon, R. D. (2006). Virtual reality exposure for veterans with posttraumatic stress disorder. *Journal of Aggression, Maltreatment & Trauma*, 12, 199–220. https://doi.org/10.1300/J146v12n01_11

Reeves, R., Elliott, A., Curran, D., Dyer, K., & Hanna, D. (2021). 360° video virtual reality exposure therapy for public speaking anxiety: a randomized controlled trial. *Journal of Anxiety Disorders*, 83, 102451. https://doi.org/10.1016/j.janxdis.2021.102451

Riva, G. (2014). Out of my real body: cognitive neuroscience meets eating disorders. *Frontiers in Human Neuroscience*, 8, 236. https://doi.org/10.3389/fnhum.2014.00236

Riva, G., Bacchetta, M., Baruffi, M., & Molinari, E. (2001). Virtual reality-based multidimensional therapy for the treatment of body image disturbances in obesity: a controlled study. *CyberPsychology & Behavior*, 4, 511–526. https://doi.org/10.1089/109493101750527079

Riva, G., Bacchetta, M., Baruffi, M., & Molinari, E. (2002). Virtual reality-based multidimensional therapy for the treatment of body image disturbances in binge eating disorders: a preliminary controlled study. *IEEE Transactions on Information Technology in Biomedicine*, 6, 224–234. https://doi.org/10.1109/titb.2002.802372

Riva, G., Bacchetta, M., Cesa, G., Conti, S., Castelnuovo, G., Mantovani, F., & Molinari, E. (2006). Is severe obesity a form of addiction? Rationale, clinical approach, and controlled clinical trial. *CyberPsychology & Behavior*, 9, 457–479. https://doi.org/10.1089/cpb.2006.9.457

Riva, G., Bacchetta, M., Cesa, G., Conti, S., & Molinari, E. (2003). Six-month follow-up in in-patient experiential cognitive therapy for binge eating disorders. *CyberPsychology & Behavior*, 6, 251–258. https://doi.org/10.1089/109493103322011533

Riva, G., Bacchetta, M., Baruffi, M., Rinaldi, S., & Molinari, E. (1998). Experiential cognitive therapy in anorexia nervosa. *Eating and Weight Disorders*, 3, 141–150. https://doi.org/10.1007/BF03340002

Rockstroh, C., Blum, J., & Göritz, A. S. (2021). A mobile VR-based respiratory biofeedback game to foster diaphragmatic breathing. *Virtual Reality*, 25, 539–552. https://doi.org/10.1007/s10055-020-00471-5

Rosenfield, N. S., Lamkin, K., Re, J., Day, K., Boyd, L., & Linstead, E. (2019). A virtual reality system for practicing conversation skills for children with autism. *Multimodal Technologies and Interaction*, 3, 28. https://doi.org/10.3390/mti3020028

Rothbaum, B. O., Hodges, L. F., Kooper, R., Opdyke, D., Williford, J. S., & North, M. (1995). Virtual reality graded exposure in the treatment of acrophobia: a case report. *Behavior Therapy*, 26, 547–554. https://doi.org/10.1016/S0005-7894(05)80100-5

Rothbaum, B. O., Hodges, L., Ready, D. J., & Alarcon, R. D. (2001). Virtual reality exposure therapy for Vietnam veterans with posttraumatic stress disorder. *Journal of Clinical Psychiatry*, 62, 617–622. https://doi.org/10.4088/JCP.v62n0808

Ruhmland, M., & Margraf, J. (2001). Efficacy of psychological treatment for specific phobia and obsessive-compulsive disorder. *Behavior Therapy*, 11, 14–26. https://doi.org/10.1159/000050321

Samnaliev, M., Noh, H. L., Sonneville, K. R., & Austin, S. B. (2014). The economic burden of eating disorders and related mental health comorbidities: an exploratory analysis using the U.S. medical expenditures panel survey. *Preventive Medicine Reports*, 2, 32–34. https://doi.org/10.1016/j.pmedr.2014.12.002

Sampaio, M., Haro, M. V. N., De Sousa, B., Melo, W. V., & Hoffman, H. G. (2021). Therapists make the switch to telepsychology to safely continue treating their patients during the COVID-19 pandemic. Virtual reality telepsychology may be next. *Frontiers in Virtual Reality*, 1, 576421. https://doi.org/10.3389/frvir.2020.576421

Sciarrino, N. A., Warnecke, A. J., & Teng, E. J. (2020). A systematic review of intensive empirically supported treatments for posttraumatic stress disorder. *Journal of Trauma Stress*, 33(4), 443–454. https://doi.org/10.1002/jts.22556

Seabrook, E., Kelly, R., Foley, F., Theiler, S., Thomas, N., Wadley, G., & Nedeljkovic, M. (2020). Understanding how virtual reality can support mindfulness practice: mixed methods study. *Journal of Medical Internet Research*, 22(3), e16106. https://doi.org/10.2196/16106

Seligman, M. E. P., & Csikszentmihalyi, M. (2000). Positive psychology: an introduction. *American Psychologist*, 55(1), 5–14. https://doi.org/10.1037/0003-066X.55.1.5

Shah, L. B. I., Torres, S., Kannusamy, P., Chng, C. M. L., & Klainin-Yobas, P. (2015). Efficacy of virtual reality-based stress management program on stress-related variables in people with mood disorders: the feasibility study. *Archives of Psychiatric Nursing*, 29, 6–13. https://doi.org/10.1016/j.apnu.2014.09.003

Simpson, H. B., Foa, E. B., Liebowitz, M. R., Huppert, J. D., Cahill, S., Maher, M. J., McLean, C. P., Bender, J., Marcus, S. M., Williams, M. T., Weaver, J., Vermes, D., Van Meter, P. E., Rodriguez, C. I., Powers, M., Pinto, A., Imms, P., Hahn, C.-G., & Campeas, R. (2013). Cognitive-behavioral therapy vs risperidone for augmenting serotonin reuptake inhibitors in obsessive-compulsive disorder: a randomized clinical trial. *JAMA Psychiatry*, 70(11), 1190–1199. https://doi.org/10.1001/jamapsychiatry.2013.1932

Sivec, H. J., & Montesano, V. L. (2012). Cognitive behavioral therapy for psychosis in clinical practice. *Psychotherapy*, 49(2), 258–270. https://doi.org/10.1037/a0028256

Smith, M. J., Bell, M. D., Wright, M. A., Humm, L. B., Olsen, D., & Fleming, M. F. (2016). Virtual reality job interview training and 6-month employment outcomes for individuals with substance use disorders seeking employment. *Journal of Vocational Rehabilitation*, 44, 323–332. https://doi.org/10.3233/JVR-160802

Södersten, P., Bergh, C., Leon, M., Brodin, U., & Zandian, M. (2017). Cognitive behavior therapy for eating disorders versus normalization of eating behavior. *Physiology & Behavior*, 174, 178–190. https://doi.org/10.1016/j.physbeh.2017.03.016

Spek, V., Cuijpers, P., Nyklícek, I., Riper, H., Keyzer, J., & Pop, V. (2007). Internet-based cognitive behavior therapy for depression and anxiety: a meta-analysis. *Psychological Medicine*, 37(3), 319–328. https://doi.org/10.1017/S0033291706008944

Stice, E. (2002). Risk and maintenance factors for eating pathology: a meta-analytic review. *Psychological Bulletin*, 128(5), 825–848. https://doi.org/10.1037//0033-2909.128.5.825

Subbalakshmi, N. K., Adhikari, P., & Jeganathan, P. S. (2014). Comparative study on cardiac autonomic modulation during deep breathing test and diaphragmatic breathing in type 2 diabetes and healthy subjects. *Journal of Diabetes Investigation*, 5, 456–463. https://doi.org/10.1111/jdi.12163

Sucala, M., Schnur, J. B., Constantino, M. J., Miller, S. J., Brackman, E. H., & Montgomery, G. H. (2012). The therapeutic relationship in e-therapy for mental health: a systematic review. *Journal of Medical Internet Research*, 14(4), e110. https://doi.org/10.2196/jmir.2084

Tashjian, V. C., Mosadeghi, S., Howard, A. R., Lopez, M., Dupuy, T., Reid, M., Martinez, B., Ahmed, S., Dailey, F., Robbins, K., Rosen, B., Fuller, G., Danovitch, I., IsHak, W., & Spiegel, B. (2017). Virtual reality for management of pain in hospitalized patients: results of a controlled trial. *JMIR Mental Health*, 4(1), e9. https://doi.org/10.2196/mental.7387

Taubin, D., Berger, A., Greenwald, D., Greenwald, H., Burke, C., Gongora, D. S., & Wilens, T. (2022). A systematic review of virtual reality therapies for substance use disorders: impact on secondary treatment outcomes. *American Journal on Addictions*, 32, 13–23. https://doi.org/10.1111/ajad.13342

Thompson, S. J., Bender, K., Lantry, J., & Flynn, P. M. (2007). Treatment engagement: building therapeutic alliance in home-based treatment with adolescents and their families. *Contemporary Family Therapy*, 29(1–2), 39–55. https://doi.org/10.1007/s10591-007-9030-6

Thorn, B. E. (2020). Putting the brain to work in cognitive-behavioral therapy for chronic pain. *Pain*, 161, S27–S35. https://doi.org/10.1097/j.pain.0000000000001839

Treasure, J. (2012). Eating disorders. *Medicine*, 40, 607–612. https://doi.org/10.1016/j.mpmed.2012.08.005

Tremain, H., McEnery, C., Fletcher, K., & Murray, G. (2020). The therapeutic alliance in digital mental health interventions for serious mental illnesses: narrative review. *JMIR Mental Health*, 7(8), e17204. https://doi.org/10.2196/17204

Usmani, S. S., Sharath, M., & Mehendale, M. (2022). Future of mental health in the metaverse. *General Psychiatry*, 35(4), e100825. https://doi.org/10.1136/gpsych-2022-100825

Utz, S. (2000). Social information processing in MUDs: the development of friendships in virtual worlds. *Journal of Online Behavior*, 1(1), 1–25.

van der Gaag, M., Valmaggia, L. R., & Smit, F. (2014). The effects of individually tailored formulation-based cognitive behavioural therapy in auditory hallucinations and delusions: a meta-analysis. *Schizophrenia Research*, 156(1), 30–37. https://doi.org/10.1016/j.schres.2014.03.016

Vass, E., Simon, V., Csukly, G., Fekete, Z., Kis, B., & Simon, L. (2022). Virtual reality-based theory of mind intervention in schizophrenia: preliminary efficacy results. *Comprehensive Psychiatry*, 119, 152350. https://doi.org/10.1016/j.comppsych.2022.152350

Ventura, S., Baños, R. M., & Botella, C. (2018). Virtual and augmented reality: new frontiers for clinical psychology. *InTech*. https://doi.org/10.5772/intechopen.74344

Wallach, H. S., Safir, M. P., & Bar-Zvi, M. (2009). Virtual reality cognitive behavior therapy for public speaking anxiety: a randomized clinical trial. *Behavior Modification*, 33, 314–338. https://doi.org/10.1177/0145445509331926

Wang, Y.-G., Liu, M.-H., & Shen, Z.-H. (2019). A virtual reality counter-conditioning procedure to reduce methamphetamine cue-induced craving. *Journal of Psychiatric Research*, 116, 88–94. https://doi.org/10.1016/j.jpsychires.2019.06.007

Wechsler, T. F., Kümpers, F., & Mühlberger, A. (2019). Inferiority or even superiority of virtual reality exposure therapy in phobias? – A systematic review and quantitative meta-analysis on randomized controlled trials specifically comparing the efficacy of virtual reality exposure to gold standard in vivo exposure in agoraphobia, specific phobia, and social phobia. *Frontiers in Psychology*, 10, 1758. https://doi.org/10.3389/fpsyg.2019.01758

Weck, F., Grikscheit, F., Jakob, M., Höfling, V., & Stangier, U. (2015). Treatment failure in cognitive-behavioural therapy: therapeutic alliance as a precondition for an adherent and competent implementation of techniques. *British Journal of Clinical Psychology*, 54(1), 91–108. https://doi.org/10.1111/bjc.12063

Weerdmeester, J., van Rooij, M. M., Engels, R. C., & Granic, I. (2020). An integrative model for the effectiveness of biofeedback interventions for anxiety regulation: viewpoint. *Journal of Medical Internet Research*, 22(7), e14958. https://doi.org/10.2196/14958

Wiebe, A., Kannen, K., Selaskowski, B., Mehren, A., Thöne, A.-K., Pramme, L., Blumenthal, N., Li, M., Asché, L., Jonas, S., Bey, K., Schulze, M., Steffens, M., Pensel, M. C., Guth, M., Rohlfsen, F., Ekhlas, M., Lügering, H., Fileccia, H., Pakos, J., Lux, S., Philipsen, A., & Braun, N. (2022). Virtual reality in the diagnostic and therapy for mental disorders: a systematic review. *Clinical Psychology Review*, 98, 102213. https://doi.org/10.1016/j.cpr.2022.102213

Wiederhold, B. K., & Wiederhold, M. D. (2005). The effect of presence on virtual reality treatment. In B. K. Wiederhold & M. D. Wiederhold (Eds.), *Virtual reality therapy for anxiety disorders: Advances in evaluation and treatment* (pp. 77–86). American Psychological Association. https://doi.org/10.1037/10858-006

Wiederhold, B. K., Gao, K., Sulea, C., & Wiederhold, M. D. (2014). Virtual reality as a distraction technique in chronic pain patients. *Cyberpsychology, Behavior, and Social Networking*, 17(6), 346–352. https://doi.org/10.1089/cyber.2014.0207

Williams, A. C., Eccleston, C., & Morley, S. (2012). Psychological therapies for the management of chronic pain (excluding headache) in adults. *Cochrane Database Systematic Reviews*, 11(11). https://doi.org/10.1002/14651858.CD007407.pub3

Wolitzky-Taylor, K. B., Horowitz, J. D., Powers, M. B., & Telch, M. J. (2008). Psychological approaches in the treatment of specific phobias: a meta-analysis. *Clinical Psychology Review*, 28(6), 1021–1037. https://doi.org/10.1016/j.cpr.2008.02.007

Wu, J., Sun, Y., Zhang, G., Zhou, Z., & Ren, Z. (2021). Virtual reality-assisted cognitive behavioral therapy for anxiety disorders: a systematic review and meta-analysis. *Frontiers in Psychiatry*, 12, 575094. https://doi.org/10.3389/fpsyt.2021.575094

Yang, C. (2023). Using cognitive therapy to explore the potential application of traditional therapy and metaverse therapy from a cognitive perspective. In *SHS Web of Conferences* (Vol. 171, p. 01030). EDP Sciences.

Index

A

Acceptance and commitment therapy (ACT), 105, 127
Accessibility, 31, 34–35
Accessories, 42–43
Addiction, 99–101
Adoption readiness model, 18
Affordability and accessibility, 27–28
Agoraphobia, 62
AI-based cue generation, 121
Allocentric Lock Theory, 80–82
Alogia, 84
Ambisonics, 116
American Psychiatric Association, 60, 62, 68
Anhedonia, 84
Anorexia nervosa, 70
Anxiety-avoidance cycle, 54
Anxiety disorders
  agoraphobia, 62
  description, 59–60
  eating disorders, 70–73
  OCD, 63–67
  panic disorder, 61–62
  PTSD, 62–63
  social anxiety disorder, 60–61
  specific phobias, 60
  SUDs, 68–70
Apple Vision Pro, 40
AppliedVR software, 127
Arachnophobia (spider phobia), 122
Arm bands, 43
AR/MR technology
  embracing, 125–126
  partial incorporation, 126–127
  roadmap summary, 124, 125
Artificial intelligence (AI) software, 120
Audio innovations, 116
Auditory hallucinations, 85
Auditory verbal hallucinations (AVH), 87–89
Augmented/mixed *vs.* virtual reality
  descriptions, applications and examples, 37
  XR technologies, 36, 37
Augmented reality (AR), 37–38
Autism spectrum disorders (ASD), 95
  age-matched controls, 96
  characteristics, 95
  DSM-5 levels, 95
  emotions and emotional intensity, 97
  likelihood of cybersickness, 98
  multisensory interactive experiences, 96
  OpenSimulator, 97
  social problem-solving tasks, 97
  social scenarios, 98
  SST, 96
  virtual settings, 96
  VR-SCT, 97–98
Avatar
  user's identity in VR world, 31
  virtual therapeutic groups, 32
AVATAR therapy (AT), 88, 128
Avolition, 84

B

Beeping machines, 78
Behavioural activation worksheet, 107
Binaural audio, 116
Binge-eating disorder, 70
Biofeedback, 102
  driven dynamic environment loop, 122
Biofeedback sensors, 121–122
  accessories, 42–43
  device, type of data collected, sensor type and information provided, 40, 41
  ECG, 41
  EDA, 41
  EEG, 40–41
  EMG, 41
  eye-tracking devices, 42
  multiple devices, 42
  respiration rate and depth, 41–42
Body distortions, 70
Body mass index (BMI), 82
Bulimia nervosa, 70

C
Cancer treatment providers, 78
Cave Automatic Virtual Environment (CAVE), 110
CBT for psychosis (CBTp), 85
C2Care software, 120, 127
Chronic pain, 79–80
Clinical checklist, 14
Cognitive-behavioural therapy (CBT), 8–9, 51. *see also* Anxiety disorders
Cognitive restructuring, 75–76
Cognitive training interventions, 13
  mental health conditions, 74
  pain management, 76–80
  people with chronic pain, 74
  physical sensations, 74
  restructuring, 75–76
Complete VR therapy, 127–128
Computer-generated VEs
  customisable, 47
  description, 46
  psychological conditions, 46
Confidentiality
  ethical considerations framework, 26
  internet-based psychotherapy, 25
  virtual psychotherapeutic interventions, 25–26
Co-therapy, 5
Cues
  anxiety-avoidance cycle, 54
  CBT thought error cycle, 55
  exposure therapy, 68
  objects, bodily sensations and situations, 53

D
Depression
  behavioural activation, 92
  cognitive restructuring, 93
  description, 92
  virtual activities and games, 93
Dialectical behaviour therapy (DBT), 105, 127
Diaphragmatic breathing, 102
Display and visual enhancements, 112
Distraction techniques, 77–79
Dynamic environments, 119
  adaptive scenarios, 120
  AI-based cue generation, 121
  biofeedback sensors, 121–122
  psychotherapy-specific, 120

E
'EARTH of well-being,' 106
Eating disorders, 70–73, 80–84
Ecological validity, 68
Effective exposure therapy, 112
Electrocardiogram (ECG), 41
Electrodermal activity (EDA), 41
Electroencephalography (EEG), 40–41
Electromyography (EMG), 41
Electronic therapy (e-therapy), 19
Elements of metaverse
  accessibility, 34–35
  avatar, 31–32
  generalisability, 34
  immersion, 33
  perspectives, 33–34
  presence, 32–33
  therapeutic outcomes, 31, 32
Emotional numbness, 63
Emotion processing theory, 56
Emotion regulation
  biofeedback training, 102
  diaphragmatic breathing, 102
  early stages of psychotherapy, 101
  guided imagery, 103
  mental health conditions, 101
  PMR, 103
  relaxation training, 101–102
Experiential Cognitive Therapy (ExCT), 81, 82
Exposure and response prevention (ERP), 64
Exposure therapy, 7–8, 56
  diagnostic category, fear and exposure concepts, 59
  early adopters, 58
  imaginal and in vivo exposures, 57
  objective (physiological) and subjective distress, 58
  physiological indicators of distress, 58
  researchers, 58
  traditional, 57
Extended reality (XR) technologies, 36
Eye-movement desensitisation and reprocessing therapy (EMDR), 127
Eye-tracking devices, 42

F
Field of view (FOV), 112
Flying phobias, 60
Full-body illusion (FBI), 82, 84, 128
Furniture-fitting app, 37

G
Gate-control theory, 76–77
Generalisability, 31, 34
Google Cardboard, 38
Guided imagery, 103

H
Habituation, 56
Hand-held controllers, 42
Hand tracking, 114–115
Haptic feedback
  accessories, 42
  devices, 115–116
Haptic vests, 43
Hardware options, 111
Headsets
  Apple Vision Pro, 40
  HTC Vive Pro 2, 40
  Meta Quest 3, 39
  PlayStation VR2, 39
  special features and prices, 39
  virtual experiences, 38
Health Insurance Portability and Accountability Act (HIPAA), 17
High-resolution visual displays, 112
Homework of VR, 11–12
Hospital noise, 78
HTC Vive, 111
Hushed conversations, 78

I
Immersion in VR, 33
Informed consent
  eye strain and visual discomfort, 11
  motion sickness and discomfort, 10
Inhibitory learning, 56
In-person therapy, 19–20
In-person *vs.* remote delivery
  traditional psychotherapy, 18–20
  VR psychotherapy, 20–22
Instagram filters, 37
Interactive objects, 120
Internet-based psychotherapy, 25
Interoceptive exposures, 61

L
Leg and foot bands, 43

M
Meta Quest 3, 39
Microsoft HoloLens, 37–38
Mindfulness, 9–10
  ACT and DBT, 105
  definition, 104
  positive emotional experiences and well-being, 104–105
Mindfulness-based stress reduction (MBSR), 127
Mixed reality (MR), 37–38
Motion sickness and discomfort, 10
Multimodal Adaptive Social Intervention in Virtual Reality (MASI-VR), 90

N
Negative symptoms of schizophrenia spectrum, 84

O
Obsessive-compulsive disorder (OCD)
  case example, 66–67
  description, 63–64
  ERP, 64
  multi-sensory experience, 65
  researchers, 64–65
Oculus Quest, 113
Olfactory accessories, 43
Oncology, 77

P
Pain management, 9
  chronic pain, 79–80
  distraction techniques, 77–79
  gate-control theory, 76–77
Panic disorder, 61–62
Panic disorder with agoraphobia (PDA), 45–46
Patient engagement and motivation, 124
Persecutory delusions, 85, 86–87
Perspectives, 33–34
Phone Goggles, 38

Pixels per inch (PPI), 112
PlayStation VR2, 39
Pleasant Events Schedule, 46
Pokémon Go, 37
Portability and comfort, VR systems, 116–117
Positive affect, 106–107
Positive symptoms of schizophrenia spectrum, 84
Post-session relaxation, 104
Post-traumatic stress disorder (PTSD), 7, 62–63
Post-VR disorientation, 11
Presence in VR, 32–33
Privacy and security concerns, 11
Progressive muscle relaxation (PMR), 103
Psychotherapy service delivery, 16
Psychotic disorders
  AVH, 87–89
  executive functioning deficits, 89–91
  persecutory delusions, 86–87
  schizophrenia spectrum, 84–85
PsyTech VR software, 120, 127
Public speaking anxiety (PSA), 45

R

Relaxation training, 101–102
  mindfulness, 104–106
  positive affect, 106–107
  and stress reduction, 10
  VR applications, 103–104
Resolution, 112

S

Safety and emergencies, 28
Savouring Beliefs Inventory (SBI), 106
Schizophrenia spectrum, 84
Skills training
  addiction, 99–101
  autism (*see* Autism spectrum disorders (ASD))
  with role-playing, 95
Social anxiety disorder (SAD), 21, 60–61
Social skills training (SST), 9, 96
Socratic questioning, 81
Specific phobias, 60
Substance use disorders (SUDs), 68–70
Substantial research, 105–106

T

Therapeutic alliance, 5–6
Therapeutic relationships
  alliance, 5–6
  anonymity, 4
  co-therapy, 5
  digital self-preservation, 5
  implications with patient, 6–7
  mental health symptoms, 4
Therapy sessions, 3
  effective therapy, 4
  traditional therapy techniques, 3
Thera VR Inc. software, 127
Tracking and input methods, 113–114
Traditional psychotherapy, 18–20

U

Unforeseen consequences, 29

V

Veterans Administration in the United States, 16
Vibration platforms, 43
Video-based VE
  clinical practice, 46
  clinicians, 44
  computer-generated, 44
  individually tailored exposures, 45
  PDA, 45–46
  Pleasant Events Schedule, 46
  PSA, 45
  psychotherapeutic interventions, 45
  realistic/cartoonish stimuli, 45
  social anxiety disorder, 45
Videoconferencing, 16
Virtual environment (VE)
  clinicians, 48, 49
  computer-generated, 46–47
  definition, 44
  platforms, 47
  type, description, advantages and disadvantages, 48
  video-based, 44–46
Virtual exposures, 63
Virtually Better software, 127
Virtual psychotherapeutic interventions, 25–26
Virtual reality exposure therapy (VRET), 20

Virtual reality job interview training (VR-JIT), 100
Virtual Reality Social Cognition Training (VR-SCT), 97–98
Virtual sessions, 83
VR dependence, 11
VR psychotherapy
  barriers, 22–23
  emotional distress, 22
  mental health practitioners, 20
  participants, 20
  SAD, 21
  safe and effective, 21
  virtual coach, 21
  VRET, 20

W
World Health Organization, 128

X
XRHealth software, 120, 127

For Product Safety Concerns and Information please contact our EU representative GPSR@taylorandfrancis.com
Taylor & Francis Verlag GmbH, Kaufingerstraße 24, 80331 München, Germany

www.ingramcontent.com/pod-product-compliance
Lightning Source LLC
LaVergne TN
LVHW050600061026
849616LV00031B/358
* 9 7 8 1 0 3 2 5 5 9 3 5 3 *